NICHOLAS PERRIN, Ph.D.

THE EXODUS
REVEALED

ISRAEL'S JOURNEY FROM SLAVERY
TO THE PROMISED LAND

D1468686

Faith
Words

New York • Boston • Nashville

FaithWords
Hachette Book Group
1290 Avenue of the Americas
New York, NY 10104
www.faithwords.com

Produced with the assistance of Livingstone, the publishing services division of the Barton-Veerman Company (www.livingstonecorp.com). Project staff includes Dave Veerman, Linda Taylor, Larry Taylor, and Nancy Nehmer.

Scripture quotations marked KJV are taken from the King James Version.

Printed in the United States of America

First Edition: October 2014

10 9 8 7 6 5 4 3 2 1

FaithWords is a division of Hachette Book Group, Inc.
The FaithWords name and logo are trademarks of Hachette Book Group, Inc.

The Hachette Speakers Bureau provides a wide range of authors for speaking events. To find out more, go to www.hachettespeakersbureau.com or call (866) 376-6591.

The publisher is not responsible for websites (or their content) that are not owned by the publisher.

ISBN: 978-1-4555-6065-3

TABLE OF CONTENTS

ABOUT THE AUTHOR

Nicholas Perrin (Ph.D., Marquette University) is Dean of the Wheaton Graduate School where he also holds the Franklin S. Dyrness Chair of Biblical Studies. He received in B.A. from The John Hopkins University, and his M.Div. from Covenant Theological Seminary. Between 2000 and 2003, he was research assistant for N. T. Wright and has since authored and edited numerous articles and books, including *Thomas and Tatian* (Society of Biblical Literature/Brill); *Thomas: The Other Gospel* (Westminster John Knox); *Lost in Transmission: What We Can Know about the Words of Jesus* (Thomas Nelson); and *Jesus the Temple* (SPCK; Baker Academic), the first of a three-part trilogy on the historical Jesus. He is also co-editor of the recently revised edition of *Dictionary of Jesus and the Gospels* (InterVarsity). Also see the companion book to this one, *Finding Jesus in the Exodus* (FaithWords).

INTRODUCTION

A friend of mine has a "Far Side" coffee mug on which is displayed a colorful cartoon depicting Moses and an apparently hesitant group of Israelites standing before a freshly parted Red Sea. The caption, conveying Moses' words to the people, reads: "What do you mean it's a bit icky?!" I love that mug. It brings out and throws into sharp relief an element of the human heart that we know all too well: small-minded ingratitude. No sooner do we recognize God for having done something extraordinary in our lives than we start harboring second thoughts and focus in on the details of what *could* be better about God's provision.

At the same time, the mug also raises an interesting historical question. When Moses parted the Red Sea on the night of the Exodus, assuming that the exposed mudflats were indeed "a bit icky," just how icky were they? Did the crossing Israelites sink ankle-deep in the mud bottom, or was there much less moisture than that, allowing them to walk along on virtually arid ground? And if you were there, would you have actually met members of the Israelite party who, frightened at the prospect of walking between the parted waters, had to be talked into it? And if so, what would they have said about the icky bottom? Nothing at all? Maybe, for all we know, some Israelites, perhaps small children, could not help but comment on the ick-factor of the Red Sea floor. We will never know. There is a lot that we will never know about the Exodus. But we can pay close attention to what we *do* know from the biblical text and employ along the way a *historically responsible imagination*.

Let me unpack that last phrase. First of all, by "historically responsible," I refer to that which is answerable to the constraints of history. Simply put: As readers of the Bible, we have to take its contents seriously as *history*. Now before you nod too quickly in agreement, let me explain exactly what I mean. Over the years, I have met countless Christians who agree with the authority of the Bible in principle and agree that its contents "really happened" but at the same time do not really take the story of the Bible seriously as history. Here's how I know. Because when they talk about things like the Ten Plagues or the parting of the Red Sea, I realize that they often have not allowed themselves to ask good questions of the text, questions such as, "When God sent plagues of various animals, was the choice of animal completely arbitrary?" or "Do the laws of hydrodynamics actually allow for the theoretical possibility of the sea parting?" Time and time again I am astonished when I meet people who, despite being extremely well educated, highly successful in their fields, and intellectually curious in regards to "real world" issues, fail to get beyond a second-grade level in terms of their understanding of biblical history. Regarding all things biblical, it is as if they are intellectually stuck in Miss Magillacutty's Sunday school class from thirty or forty years ago.

The truth is that Miss Magillacutty never encouraged you to ask, "Do the laws of hydrodynamics actually allow for the theoretical possibility of a sea parting?" Of course that wasn't her fault. She was just doing her job, spiritually nurturing you when you were still learning to tie your shoes. But perhaps you have picked up this book because you realize you need to go deeper. The Apostle Paul says, "When I was a child, I thought like a child and I reasoned like a child; when I became an adult, I put an end to childish things" (1 Corinthians 13:11). Perhaps you are reading this book because you want to get past childish ways of thinking in considering the Exodus. If this happens to be you, you should be commended. Whether you are casually interested or highly interested in the Exodus, I believe that undertaking learning projects like these are just part of what it means to love God with your mind. While this book certainly cannot answer all of the questions raised by the second book of the Bible, it will be, I hope, a good start.

Let me come back to the phrase, "historically responsible imagination" and focus on the last word of the phrase. Sometimes folks get nervous with the word *imagination*. They want (with echoes of Sergeant Joe Friday) "just the facts, Ma'am." They might say, "Don't muddy the waters by bringing imagination into it." I want to push back on this line of thinking; I want to engage people's imagination about the Exodus. The best way I know how to do this is to engage my own imagination a bit and then talk about it. Some say that this means taking liberties with the text. But the very nature of reading the Bible actually requires us to connect dots, and once we begin to connect the dots, we are using our imagination.

When I was first approached to write this book, I confess I was hesitant. I thought to myself, "My specialty has been in the New Testament and not so much in the Old Testament" (although I would also say, "Show me a New Testament scholar who doesn't know his or her way around the Old Testament, and I might as well show you a plumber who doesn't know his or her way around pipes"). I am well aware that a good number of scholars have logged far more hours than I in studying the Exodus. At the same time, I also realize that such scholarship has not done a lot to connect the dots on an imaginative level, at least not when it comes to this part of the Bible. Again, I'm not talking about wild, unbridled imagination. But sometimes thinking things through in a self-disciplined way can be helpful, asking: "What would it have been like if I were there?" Perhaps the scholarly and semi-scholarly genres tend to discourage such ruminations. As a rule, we academics don't like the thought of starting out to write a serious scholarly work only to find that we have blended genres by lapsing into an exercise in Ignatian spirituality. In this book, I am an unrepentant rule-breaker and genre blender. My hope is to bring the results of cutting-edge scholarship on the Exodus to bear on how we imagine it historically. When we do, I believe we end up with more interesting questions.

This should not deprive us of theological reflection but, rather, should help set the stage for it. And that, I think, is the final reason why I believe this book needed to be written: to offer a lay-accessible work that speaks to the theological significance of the Exodus. Again, since this book is primarily about history, I don't assume any faith persuasion on the part of its readers. At the same time, however, I suspect that a good number of this book's readers will be interested in occasionally connecting the dots from the Old Testament to the New Testament, and from Old Testament history to modern-day practice. For those who want to go beyond only occasionally connecting these dots, I would recommend the sequel to the present volume, *Finding Jesus in the Exodus*. In the meantime, in the present volume, we will largely have our feet anchored to the sands of Egypt and Sinai, with our theological Ray-Bans fixed firmly on the brim of our noses. No Torah-reading Jew of antiquity would have dreamed of reading about the Exodus without doing theology. Perhaps we could benefit by following suit.

Before entering into the subject matter, I wish to register several notes in regards to the biblical text and the history of this pivotal event. First, unless otherwise stated, all biblical translations from the Hebrew and Greek are my own. I have done this to provide a certain freshness to the study, although of course those who have little familiarity with the text will hardly know the difference! I have also done this so as to render the text in a slightly more colloquial way, at least compared to most major translations.

Second, while I am well aware that the proper dating of the Exodus is a much-debated topic (an "early Exodus" dating in fifteenth century B.C. *versus* a "late Exodus" dating in the thirteenth century B.C. *versus* "no Exodus"—a minimalist view within the academy that holds the Exodus to be holy fiction), for the purposes of the book I have very intentionally decided (1) to rule out the third option ahead of time and (2) to refuse to adjudicate between the first two options. This is partly because I believe that the debate between an "early Exodus" and a "late Exodus" would distract from my purposes; this is partly because I believe a strong case can be and has been made on both sides. We should, accordingly, also give due respect to both sides. While some advocates for an early Exodus have framed this as a battle between what the Good Book says and what craven archaeologists say (given the lack of material evidence for an early Exodus), this is simply an unfortunate and unfair construal. In truth, the issue is complex and will perhaps remain intractably so. Having no intention of making my own case either way, I will leave it to curious readers, interested in settling out on this question, to do their own homework with an open mind and a good dose of intellectual humility. Wherever you stand or don't stand on this issue, this book will still be for you.

The third note has to do with contemporary source-critical hypothesis. Without going into too much detail, I need to inform or remind my readers (as the case may be) that modern-day scholarship around the Exodus cannot be undertaken without entering into the very complicated question of documentary sources, what biblical scholars have called J-E-D-P. These letters correspond respectively to the so-called Yahwist source (J), the Elohist source (E), the Deuteronomist (D), and the Priestly source (P). The bulk of the material in our purview belongs to the Priestly source (P). But because there are a number of methodological problems that immediately present themselves on a serious consideration of P and the other alleged sources (some of which have brought the entire paradigm to a virtual breaking point), I will bracket this entire discussion and instead strive to get to the history behind the texts. I am well aware that the issue of sources (who recorded this and when did they do so?) cannot entirely be separated from the issue of history (what actually happened?), but for the sake of simplicity, I will do just that. Again, students who wish to delve deeper into this subject are free to consult the appropriate secondary literature. That will not be our gig.

With these disclaimers in place, we are ready now to follow in Moses' footsteps. Be forewarned: his is a circuitous and winding route. If you think that the wilderness generation excelled in moving about hither and yon, the same is actually true of Moses even before he crossed the Red Sea. He got around—both in terms of geography and in terms of life. Highs and lows—he had them both. And of course, in life so do we. On some level, Moses' story is also our story.

But even more so, Moses' story is actually a story about God. This was the God of Abraham, Isaac, and Jacob. This was the God whom Moses had met at the burning bush. This was also the God who would vanquish Egypt's idols and deliver Israel. For that reason, when we follow in Moses' footsteps, we are bound to meet God. Of course meeting God and encountering God are two separate matters. Pharaoh may have met God but he never (so far as we know) encountered God the way that, say, Moses clearly did. As you read this book about the Exodus, remember that God did not ultimately give the second book of the Bible so that we might merely *meet* him but so that we might *encounter* him—more exactly, *be encountered by him*. And we are encountered through Israel's first encounter. Thus, I hope in some sense, this book will help open not only the window of history but also the window of the heart touched by the one who revealed himself as I AM. More on that name and lots of other things in the pages ahead.

PROMISE

Now then these are the names of the sons of Israel who came to Egypt with Jacob, each of them with his household: Reuben, Simeon, Levi, and Judah, Issachar, Zebulun, and Benjamin, Dan and Naphtali, Gad and Asher. The sum number of people descended from Jacob was seventy, and Joseph was already in Egypt. Then Joseph died, all his brothers, and that whole generation. But the Israelites were fruitful and grew in number; they multiplied and grew very, very strong, and as a result the land was filled with them. Now there emerged a new king over Egypt, one who did not know Joseph. He said to his people, "Look, the Israelite people are more numerous and more powerful than we are. So, let's be smart in how we deal with them, or they will increase and in the event of a war they'll ally themselves with our enemies and fight against us and escape from the land." *(Exodus 1:1–10)*

Last summer when I was spending time in Jerusalem, my oldest son and I visited the renowned Holocaust museum, Yad Vashem. Bringing my son was intentional on my part; one might say it was even a mission. My grandfather, Max Gutmann, was a German Jew whose larger family was wiped out in the Holocaust. And so, though I am a confessing Christian, a part of me identifies with the victims of the Holocaust, most of whom were, of course, Jewish. It is as if some of my roots are bound up in that event, and I want my children somehow to own that as well. I don't want them to forget. And I inwardly hope that one day they will bring their children and continue to remember, down through the generations.

We had been to this museum before. Yet every time I go, it might as well be the first time. The outrageous displays of Nazi memorabilia, the gruesome photos of human butchery, video after video of powerful interviews with Holocaust survivors—the experience never becomes old or commonplace. Nor, I suppose, should it. If it did, something would be terribly wrong. For me, remembering something like this is at once a painful process; yet, paradoxically, it is also a process that brings hope—the hope of a promise.

In my opinion, the most strategic decision in the museum design was made at the beginning of the tour. Here one finds no pictures of orphaned children or firing squads but instead images of ordinary European Jews as they went about their daily and ordinary lives *before* the Holocaust. They were singing, playing music, laughing—living life. Then, suddenly, very suddenly, as one progresses through the displays, the mood turns dark. In due course, we move from Hitler's rise to power to the infamous Night of the Broken Glass, to the establishment of the death camps, and on to the rest of the unspeakable atrocities. In one moment, life for the Jews seemed so simple and unencumbered. But then seemingly overnight, all that changed. We ask ourselves, "How on earth did this happen?"

How Did This Happen?

I suspect that this is much the same question the ancestors of many of these same Jews were asking some three and a half millennia ago. The sons of Israel were resident aliens in the eastern Delta region of Egypt where they had been for years. They had settled there in order to avoid famine and starvation in their native land of Canaan. When they first arrived, they were warmly welcomed due to their connection to Joseph, Egypt's hero from abroad. Then, almost precipitously, the reception cooled. And "cooled" turned into cold. Soon enough, the Israelites found themselves in a bad spot on every level. One might even have called it a crisis.

We tend to think of crises as situations that force some kind of decision or decisive outcome. But the situation in which the Israelites had found themselves was nothing like that. The Israelites probably had no identifiable turning point when they could look back and say, "Yes, that was the day that we lost favor in the eyes of the Egyptians!" Rather, the confederation of tribes had succumbed to a slow and steady deterioration of their social standing within Egyptian society—and then finally a state of slavery. As the various holocausts of the twentieth century remind us, people can go to bed one night feeling reasonably secure only to awaken the next day to find their prospects plummeting in a dizzying and perplexing free fall, all because they fell on the wrong side of an ethnic divide. Given the right public mood, the right ruler in place, and the right circumstances (or, rather, the *wrong* mood, place, and circumstances), even those who are accustomed to feel most secure within society may suddenly find their world caving in around them. This is how, more or less, it must have been with ancient Israel.

Perhaps, in the early years, the experience of the Jews residing in Egypt was similar to what has been a common experience of immigrant groups in the United States down the course of American history. The sons of Israel would have been easy enough to identify: what they wore, how they spoke, the customs they practiced, even the way they looked (assuming there were standard genetic features that set them apart from the Egyptians)—all this would have made it quite clear who "belonged here" and who was a resident alien. I imagine that when the sons of Abraham, Isaac, and Jacob walked down the road, the established Egyptian indigents recognized them right away; and a number of these, out of fear and prejudice, consciously or unconsciously decided to keep "the others" at a safe distance. When people meet other people who are conspicuously different from themselves, an all-too-common reaction is to match one's own ignorance with fear and hatred. A useful term here is *xenophobia*—a fear and dislike of foreigners. The ancient Egyptians were chronically xenophobic.

And in this case, it was a xenophobia exacerbated by a bitter and humiliating experience deeply ingrained on Egypt's national consciousness: the advent of the Hyksos in the nineteenth century B.C. The Hyksos were not so much an identifiable tribe as a conglomeration of non-Egyptians, though predominantly Canaanite. While earlier scholarship had theorized that the Hyksos had come to settle the Nile Delta region through violent means, more recent research seems to show that actually they had come to power gradually and, initially anyway, peaceably. It all began when Amenemhat III (ruled c. 1860–c. 1815 B.C.) undertook major building projects that opened up new markets for skilled and unskilled laborers. Over time, families from the Levant (the eastern seaboard of the Mediterranean between modern-day Turkey and Egypt) began to trickle in looking for gainful employment. As immigrants often do, they found one another and settled down. By 1700 B.C., the political instability of the larger surrounding region left local tribal chieftains in a position to establish their own small kingdoms in the region. Among these was the Hyksos ruler King Nehesy who set up his capital at Avaris, a city in the heart of the eastern Nile Delta. Using Avaris as a base, the Hyksos expanded. By 1674 B.C., King Salitis (a Semite who would have been identified as a Hyksos) had become established in Memphis, the ancient capital city of Egypt just to the south of the Delta region. Twenty-five years later, the Hyksos, having recognized the weakness of the reigning Egyptian dynasties, would deal the Egyptians crushing defeats, wresting control of the northern part of Egypt (Lower Egypt).

Yet the Egyptian rulers of the south were not about to let this go unchecked forever. Seqenen-re II (also known as "the Brave") was determined to use his position at Thebes (three hundred miles to the south) as a launch pad for campaigns against the Hyksos. Although "the Brave" seemed to have fallen in battle to the Hyksos (his mummified skull shows multiple trauma to the head), his sons Kamose and Amose carried the cause forward. Kamose had managed to regain the important city of Memphis; later, his brother Amose would successfully rout the Hyksos from the land altogether, sending them packing back to their original homeland of Canaan—all around 1550 B.C. After almost two centuries, the Egyptians had finally rid the land of the Hyksos, but at great national cost.

So we can see why even a century later, the great Queen Hatshepsut (ruled 1480–1469 B.C.) would order chiseled into the gate frame at one of her temples an inscription that vividly recounted the ruin brought by the "visitors" from the Levant. From that point on, all the way down to the third century B.C. (according to Egyptian historian Manetho), the Hyksos were routinely credited as being the cruelest of peoples. Evidently the Egyptians who had lived through the so-called Second Intermediate Period (1650–1550 B.C.) went on record that the Hyksos were guilty of ravaging Egypt's land and submitting its people to slavery and mass slaughter. Whether or not this report was true, as far the Egyptians were concerned, what the parents passed down to their children became the national perception, and perception was the reality. From that point on, no one would quickly forget the ruthless Semitic Hyksos who had abused Egyptian hospitality by pillaging half of Egypt.

Whether or not this two-hundred-year engagement with the foreigners occurred in the lead-up to Israel's enslavement or during it (this depends on our dating of the Exodus) does not dramatically affect my point. We need only a little historical imagination to think the Egyptians' thoughts after them. Here were the sons of Jacob, the Israelites of the eastern Delta, a Semitic people who had come to settle in the area—just like the Semitic Hyksos. Here, too, was a people whose history included stories of highly talented individuals (think Joseph) who occupied high positions of power in Egypt—just as the Hyksos had come to fill the leading administrative posts in Egypt, at least before they turned violent. And, finally, here were the Israelites noticeably multiplying (Exodus 1:7) with a population growth trajectory outstripping that of the native Egyptians. This is just where all the trouble began with the Hyksos, right under the Egyptians' noses. "Well," the Egyptians must have said to themselves, "we won't be fooled again. We'll show them!" Given the national memory and the political mood, any Egyptian ruler coming along and suggesting new policies serving to limit the Israelites' rights would only be pushing on an open door.

If these factors were not enough to arouse paranoia and indignation within the Egyptian ranks, we also have to reckon with the fact that the descendants of Israel had learned to keep to themselves and did not blend in easily or willingly with Egyptian society. In other words, if the Egyptians were averse to rubbing shoulders with the Israelites, the antipathy likely ran both ways—just how much antipathy is anyone's guess. Sociologists have long observed that members of a minority culture will naturally tend to stick together as a way of affirming and preserving their collective self-identity. If this is the way it worked for the disempowered minority of Israel, then we can only imagine that there was little possibility of Israelites being absorbed into the mainstream of Egyptian culture.

From Free to Enslaved

So much for the social background leading up to the Israelites' indenture. But how is it that the descendants of Israel went to bed one night as freedmen only to wake up the next morning to a day in which they would find themselves condemned to hard labor for no pay? According to Exodus 1, the decision came from the very top down. The new policy was to enslave the Israelites lest they "increase and, in the event of war, join our enemies and fight against us and escape from the land" (Exodus 1:10). As a result, taskmasters were appointed, and the Israelites were forced into slave labor. According to Scripture, then, Pharaoh pressed the Israelites into service because of their proliferating population. This explanation is certainly consistent with the social and political background I have been describing. It all makes sense historically.

Here is also a theological point. When we think back to the very beginning of Israel's story—that is, back to the creation story itself—we remember Yahweh's benediction and mandate to Adam and Eve: "God blessed them, and God said to them, 'Be *fruitful and multiply*, and fill the earth and subdue it; and have dominion over the fish of the sea and over the birds of the air and over every living thing that moves upon the earth'" (Genesis 1:28). The same mandate for multiplication is repeated three times in the story of Noah (Genesis 8:17; 9:1, 7). Later, when Yahweh confirms his covenant with Abraham, one of the key promises in the covenant was his progeny's fruitfulness (Genesis 17:6). Promises of fruitfulness also follow Isaac (Genesis 26:22; 28:1–4). When the patriarchs' descendants come to Goshen in the land of Egypt, they follow their forefathers' lead for "they were fruitful and multiplied exceedingly" (Genesis 47:27). Thus, when Pharaoh expresses his dismay over the expanding demographic sector known as "the Israelites," he is reacting to a well-established pattern within the biblical story that had its roots in one of Yahweh's very first commands to Israel (that is, when Israel was in Adam). The Israelites' fertility was a mark not only of their obedience to that creational mandate but also to God's blessing them even in the midst of their estranged existence. Meanwhile, as the well-versed ancient readers of Torah would have understood almost immediately, Pharaoh's resistance to this population trend made him a marked man.

Think of it: Israel's fruitfulness was a direct result of Yahweh's blessing. In attempting to impede Israel's growth as a nation, Pharaoh was in fact cursing God's people (indeed the Hebrew notion of "curse" entails the notion of restriction or confinement). Israel's God had already promised Abraham, "I will bless those who bless you, and the one who curses you I will curse" (Genesis 12:3). Again, the attentive reader would have been well aware: If Yahweh's promise to Abraham were trustworthy, then Yahweh was bound to curse the same Pharaoh who had cursed Israel.

Thus, Scripture provides a theological explanation of Pharaoh's new policy that is also historically credible. But this does not mean that it is an exhaustive explanation. The historian within us still has questions. For example, one might be forgiven for being puzzled over why the ruler of Egypt would implement such radical measures to counter Israel's growth. Even if Pharaoh noticed that Israel was expanding, it seems like quite a jump to move from this observation to saying, "Okay, let's put the lot of them under house arrest, subject them to severe slavery, and that will be that." But the jump is not impossible. After all, Pharaoh was the absolute monarch of the land. They had no Bill of Rights, no Alliance Defense Fund, no ACLU waiting to step in.

However, historians tend to prefer a plausible cause whenever they can get their hands on one.

The Ego of Rameses

One such plausible cause, if we go with a late dating of the Exodus, is the building program undertaken by Rameses II (ruled 1279–1213 B.C.) outside of Avaris. Rameses was perhaps the greatest and most powerful of all Egyptian Pharaohs. And he seems—lest there be any doubters of this in his own time—to have dedicated most of his life to proving it. He not only commandeered a fantastically huge army but also energetically dedicated himself to a great number of magnificent building and monumental projects, all of which essentially served as unmovable billboards of kingdom propaganda. An example of this is a red granite, eighty-plus-ton colossal statue of the man that today is on display in a museum. Rameses erected this and other similar statues, not because he was a narcissist (although for all we know, he was), but because it was his way of saying, as it were, "Don't mess with me."

Here's something else about Rameses: He had a shock of auburn hair—he was a red-tinted blonde. (This also happens to be my wife's hair color, but that's about as far as the comparisons between Rameses and Mrs. Perrin go.) We know this because we still have Rameses's body (and hair) intact. (In the 1970s, when Egyptologists noticed that this particular three-thousand-year-old mummified body was inexplicably beginning to deteriorate, they flew him to Paris for further investigation—complete with an Egyptian passport that listed his occupation as "King—deceased.") This is relevant because ancient Egyptians associated red hair with the god Seth. This worked out well because it turns out that Rameses's father, Sethos I, was also a devotee of Seth; thus, Sethos's name. It was almost as if Rameses was destined to be a worshipper of Seth and, in some sense, precisely because he was Pharaoh, Seth's earthly incarnation.

This was a problem for two reasons. First, if the Egyptians had anything like an official state god, that god was Atum. Second, just as all the Egyptian gods had their own regional, temple-centered bases, Atum's base was in the capital city of Thebes, to the south. Meanwhile, Seth was a god who was localized in the north, in the eastern Delta in fact. This all made for quite a conundrum with religio-political implications on all levels.

What to do? Well, Rameses knew exactly what he was going to do: He would relocate his main palace way up to the north in the eastern Delta, far away from the temple of Atum and square in the heartland of Seth. We can only imagine the Theban priests of Atum arching their eyebrows at the news. Despite the loss of social capital in the south, the move made a lot of sense. There in the eastern Delta, Rameses could solidify his connection with the local god Seth, and as an added bonus, obtain more direct access to the ongoing military campaigns being waged along the important trade corridor leading up the east coast of the Mediterranean Sea.

Lesser rulers would have attempted to appease the administrative and priestly bureaucracy back in Thebes by minimizing the move, acting as if the palace up north was nothing more than a cheap weekend-getaway cottage, but Rameses does just the opposite. He throws everything he has into the new location by extensive building projects. Perhaps this was to be expected. Judging by his legacy, Rameses does not seem to be the kind of man who did things by half measures. Of course, he would name the new capital city after himself: Pi (Per)-Ramesse Aa-Nakhtu, meaning the Domain of Rameses, Great in Victory. In a short time (*very* short time, I'm sure), the city would come to be known simply as Rameses.

But where would Pharaoh find the manpower to build such a city with the kind of speed and the kind of big splash that he was looking for? Enter the Israelites: "They set taskmasters over them to oppress them with forced labor. They built supply cities, Pithom and Rameses, for Pharaoh" (Exodus 1:11). By conscripting these people into his construction projects, Pharaoh could accomplish two objectives in one stroke: clamp down on those worrisome Is-raelites *and* get some building projects done for his personal glory.

Sitting on this side of history, we can see that the Pharaoh in the long run did not accomplish either of his objectives. Before we get halfway through the book of Exodus and by the time we get to the end of the present book, we will see that Pharaoh's plan for the Israelites sorely backfires. And as for Rameses's goal of making an enduring name for himself through a made-to-order city, well, iron-ically, today we are not even sure about its precise whereabouts. We are only slightly more confident about the spot of the other "supply city" mentioned in Exodus 1:11. Pithom (i.e., Per-'tum, House of Atum) is today marked off by the archaeological site known as Tell el-Maskhuta—we think. So much for the best-laid plans of mice, men, and Pharaohs.

Slavery and Slaves

So, what did this all mean for the ancient Israelites? Needless to say, the Pharaoh's decision was for the twelve tribes nothing less than a devastating turn of events. From that point on, Israel was in slavery. But what did that slavery look like? Although the Af-rican-American experience has looked to the oppression of the Exodus as a kind of prototype of its own journey from slavery to the Civil Rights Movement and beyond, the analogy is not exact. In terms of the historical details, we find points of comparison as well as contrast.

Let me begin with the contrasts. First of all, while antebellum slaveholders regarded their slaves as chattel for their personal use and disposal, in the Egyptian context the Israelites worked for the state, for its personal use and disposal. We have no evidence that Egyptians kept individual Israelites as house servants or field slaves. Rather, if we were to draw everything on an organizational chart, all the vertical lines would converge very quickly on the chief executive, Pharaoh. Second, whereas American slavery employed men and women, in the Egyptian scenario it is likely that only men were enslaved. After all, the record shows that Pharaoh was predominantly interested in impressed labor for the sake of his building projects, and in antiquity—as opposed to today—the business of construction and brick-making was restricted to men. Third, American pre–Civil War slavery normally entailed the dissolution of black families, where men were forcibly separated from their wives, mothers from their children, and so on. As grievous as the Israelites' bondage was, they were spared this particular sorrow. Since only men were needed, the Egyptians had no interest in disrupting the structure of the Israelite families; and judging by the institution of the family-based meal of the Passover (among other details), the Israelite families remained intact throughout the period of the oppression.

In retrospect, the preservation of Israelite family structure may have—from a human point of view—been a crucial element in Israel's deliverance. Heads of families represented the families' interests to the clan, and clan leaders represented their constituencies' interests to the tribe, and each tribe could represent their own interest in respect to one another. For Moses to lead Israel as a whole group apart from its having this kind of unofficial, representational, self-governance system in place would have been impossible. Most of us, when we read of Moses' struggles to "herd the cats" through the Sinai wilderness, tend to imagine a beleaguered man, maybe looking something like Gandalf, being shouted down by an unruly mob of thousands upon thousands. In reality, however, Moses most likely worked with the key leaders who represented those thousands upon thousands, unruly as they were. And while even Moses had days when he wished for different leaders to work with, he must have also known how much more difficult life would have been without them. Apart from Yahweh's sovereign preservation of the family unit, Moses would have faced the impossible task of mobilizing a virtual anarchy.

Having laid out some of the differences between the Israelites' enslavement (as best as we can reconstruct it) and the African-American experience of slavery, let me cite some similarities. First of all, just as antebellum slaveholders often held their slaves to exacting quotas of production (as witnessed, for example, in the book and film *Twelve Years a Slave*), the same held true in ancient Egypt. Second, we have historical documentation from both periods that when the slaves did not meet their prescribed quotas, the results would be physical punishment—sometimes severe punishment. One ancient text describes the plight of the Egyptian fieldworker as follows:

> Then the scribe lands on the bank to receive the harvest, his followers carry sticks and the men carry palm rods. They say, "Give us corn"—there is none there. Then they beat him as he lies stretched out and bound on the ground, they throw him into

the canal and he sinks down, head under water.
His wife is bound before his eyes and his children
are put in fetters. (A. Erman, *Life in Ancient Egypt*
[New York: Dover, 1971], p. 445)

Whereas most of us hold jobs where our superiors may motivate us through some combination of the carrot and the stick, slavery has no "carrot." Meanwhile, the stick, a literal stick, is ubiquitous. For both American slavery and Israelite slavery, horrific but true, the daily dread of failing to meet one's quotas and regular beatings were a way of life.

The life of a construction worker in Egypt was hard. While many of the monuments that tourists are still able to see today are made from quarried stone, most of the edifices built in ancient Egypt were made of mud-brick, itself a combination of water from the Nile, mud from its banks, and straw from the fields. Because water was key, the worksite needed to be located near a pool of water or a canal leading away from the Nile. Some workers would then be appointed simply to transport water mixed with clay back and forth all day. Others would collect the stubble from the fields to give the bricks body. Still others would take these ingredients and mold bricks, either by hand or with the help of a wooden mold. Once the brick was shaped, it was laid out to dry in the sun along with the others where it was left for three days. At that point, the brick would have to be flipped over so that the other side could also get sun exposure and a proper drying out. The process took about a week.

Brick-making was a time-intensive and human-resource-intensive process. As the Egyptians were master builders, the relatively easy part was putting the bricks where they belong; the hard part, and the potential bottleneck of any building operation, was the production of the bricks themselves. As a result, the Israelite brick-makers drew the scrutinizing gaze of any Egyptian foreman wanting to get the job done, properly and quickly (or else!). We have a leather scroll from roughly the year 1300 B.C. referring to an 80,000-brick quota for forty men in the course of a day. This makes two thousand bricks per man per day. On the supposition that each laborer worked a twelve-hour work day with absolutely no breaks, this would require an output of a brick every twenty seconds. On the assumption that each brick maker had to find his own mud, add it to the mold, shape it, punch it out of the mold, and lay it out to dry in an unoccupied spot alongside countless other bricks, this made for an unimaginably fast clip on any scenario. Needless to say, the same scroll mentions that all forty men failed to achieve the quota. We can imagine that punitive beatings ensued.

As if these kinds of pressures were not enough, the work was also, the ancient sources tell us, agonizing. Surprisingly, one of the difficult aspects of the job, again according to ancient record, was the constant exposure to a stiff wind on the Delta. The ancient texts enumerate other challenges: the constant carting of extremely heavy materials under the hot Egyptian sun, the repetitive strain disorders that would inevitably result (often detectable on the exhumed skeletal remains of ancient slaves), and the ongoing unpleasantness of being caked in Nile mud all day—remember that the opportunity for taking a bath was rare indeed. Assuming that these slaves worked seven days a week, one has to suspect that given the strains of such work, life expectancy was correspondingly shortened.

Adding Insult to Injury

Here's another piece: the religious or theological significance of the Israelites' assigned construction task. Recall the names of the cities in which the Israelites were put to work: Pithom and Rameses. The first was centered on the god Atum; the second, on the god Seth. Atum was the Egyptian creator god, the first god from which all other lower-ranking gods derived. Seth was the god of the desert; he also murdered his brother, Osiris, god of the afterlife. The Israelite slaves knew that when they were going to work on Pharaoh's buildings, they were not only working for the top brass of Egypt but also, by extension, the gods. While we have little way of gauging the depth of the Israelites' faith in the God of their forefathers, I believe we can be sure that any Jews who thought that they were serving the true Creator God must have been extremely frustrated in being consigned to spend the best years of their short lives building pagan temples. Being forced to work was one thing; it was another to be forced to work on the temple of the usurper of the true Creator God, the God of Abraham. If the beatings, brutal labor, and mud were not demeaning enough, the indignity of having to serve another people's idea of a Creator God only added to the strain.

In seeking to compare the Israelites' experience with anything remotely similar to my own experience, I suppose the best I could possibly do is think back to the most physically demanding job I ever had. I had just graduated from college and was planning to start work with a campus ministry organization at a Maryland state school in August. Meanwhile, during an unusually hot June and July, I decided to make a few dollars by working for a New Jersey horse farmer named Joe Marino. Joe was a tough man who held high expectations for his hired hands. One of the projects Joe put me onto was building a very long and winding rail fence to create a corral. This first meant taking a manual posthole digger and creating dozens of holes for the fence posts (believe me, if you've never done this, it's much harder than it sounds). When my hands got too sore to keep digging postholes, Joe would send me up to the upper hayloft where I would move bales of hay from one end of the loft to the other, and then throw them out of the loft onto a pickup parked on the ground below. Of course, if the temperature was in the upper 90s in the shade, who knows what the temperature must have been in an unventilated hayloft. I can remember being so tired that when I got home at the end of a day, I would sometimes just go right to bed, only to turn around and do it all over again the next day. On my last day of work when Joe and I said our goodbyes, he said to me with a grin, "Nick, when you go to Maryland and tell them about hell, tell them, '*I've* been there. *I've* worked for Joe Marino!'"

Of course, working for Joe wasn't hell. It was very tough work, but it earned good money. I always had the option of quitting. Besides, if I didn't dig enough holes or bale enough hay, no one was going to beat me. I was still a free agent; at the end of each workday, I simply hopped dusty and sweaty into the car and went where I wanted to go. Finally, it was not as if Joe was asking me to dig postholes for columns framing out a new building for the god of the Flying Spaghetti Monster Church. In other words, I felt no inherent tension between my faith and the demands of my assigned task.

The Israelites had none of these advantages. They did not earn any money and, of course, had no option of quitting. If they didn't show up to work, either they or their families would suffer the consequences. As a result of Pharaoh's edict, therefore, the Israelite men would henceforth be banished to grinding out this miserable existence, sacrificing their lives on the altar of a foreign god. How their families were sustained—whether they were subsidized by Pharaoh or left to fend for themselves—is unclear. When all the Israelite fathers had to wake up to new aches and pains each morning in order to spend yet another long backbreaking day at work on Pharaoh's buildings—just as their fathers had done, and their fathers before them, just as their sons were doomed to do, and their sons after them—hope must have seemed so very dim. Obviously, this also would have been no picnic for the mothers at home who somehow had to make it all work without their husbands.

The Promise

So I wonder, much as I wondered at Yad Vashem, what keeps people going in situations like those? What keeps them alive? Was it their families? Was it a vague hope for a better future? Was it simply the will to survive? I'm sure the answer varies from person to person, even as does the resolve to keep going in such times. I'm sure the answer also varied from person to person in the Israelites' situation, too.

Still the Israelites had something very powerful: They had the promise of their God. While some biblical scholars might dispute the possibility of the Israelites having access to the promises spelled out to Abraham in Genesis 15, I believe that the kind of story we read about in Genesis 15 would be just the kind of story parents would want their children to know and pass on. Almost as part of their mission as parents, they transmitted such stories orally, all as part of their determination to remain the people of God. Such stories included the oral tradition of Abraham's vision, which preserved the promise that the tribes would be oppressed for centuries but eventually come out of the land with great possessions (Genesis 15:13–14). The reason they *had* to come out was so that they could be a blessing to the nations (Genesis 12:2–3). Although they served Pharaoh, as well as the gods of Atum and Seth in the present time, they looked forward to the day when their God would rescue them. This was all bound up in the promise, a promise which ultimately entailed blessings for all the nations. Freedom—the freedom to worship the God of Abraham—was their destiny. The promise of this same God held forth nothing less.

What the Israelites needed was deliverance from an impossible situation. What they needed was release from their political, social, economic, and spiritual oppression. Such redemption was necessary, not because they believed in "life, liberty and the pursuit of happiness"; nor was it because they felt inwardly committed to democracy, equality, or even human rights. The Israelites believed that their God was the Creator God and that they had been chosen to play a key role in the Creator's purposes. Their destiny was to serve as the agents of the Abrahamic blessing. The Creator God, Abraham's God, had said that the world would be blessed through the seed, so they had been faithful in multiplying despite Pharaoh's threats.

Now they could only work, pray, and wait. And as years gave way to decades and the decades piled up, the generations came and went. Still they waited and prayed some more—all under the taskmaster's rod. And all the while they held on to the promise made to Abraham. Little did they know that their God would make good on that promise by sending a man. More about him in the next chapter.

PRINCE AND PARIAH

So Pharaoh commanded all his people, "Every Hebrew son that is born you shall throw into the Nile, but you must let every girl live." Now a man from the house of Levi went and married a Levite woman. The woman became pregnant and bore a son; and when she saw her fine baby boy, she hid him for three months. When she could hide him no longer she found a papyrus basket for him, and coated it with tar and pitch; she put the child in it and positioned it among the reeds on the bank of the river. (Exodus 1:22—2:3)

One day while on a trip, our family of four decided to stop for lunch in Corbin, Kentucky. Whenever I'm in the South, I always want to make a beeline to the nearest barbeque establishment. As a Yankee, I first became attached to barbeque when I moved to St. Louis—where I met and courted my wife—and discovered along the way a handful of remarkable barbeque restaurants. Sometimes Southerners will claim that the North has no good barbeque places, for example, in places like Chicago where we currently live. That's not true. They are just few and far between. Still, to this day, whenever we visit my St. Louis-based in-laws over a weekend, we try to visit the very church where Bob gave me Camie's hand in marriage, and stop for barbeque.

Entering Corbin, I was beginning to realize that we had a problem—more exactly, *I* had a problem. As invariably happens when our family tries to eat lunch on the road, we had a hung jury on the issue of where to eat. It came down to BBQ versus KFC. It was my fault this time. I had made the mistake of informing my wife and children that the very first Kentucky Fried Chicken restaurant happened to be "right here in Corbin, Kentucky!" That's right. "More than that," I told them, "there's also a museum that goes with it." This turned out to be a classic case of issuing too much information.

I really should have remembered just how partial my boys were to the Colonel's chicken. For one of them, *not* to eat at the very first KFC in the world, well, that would be like a highly devout Catholic on her first trip to Mexico City *not* visiting the shrine of the Virgin of Guadalupe. When my wife chimed in that paying our respects to the man with the white suit and black string tie would be a good idea, I knew I had been outvoted. Honestly, I don't think she really wanted to go; I think she would have preferred barbeque. Sometimes a mother will make just about any personal sacrifice for her sons.

Lunch was decent; the museum dedicated to the Colonel was fascinating. Surely, I had always unconsciously believed that, with a franchise as successful as KFC, the Colonel must have dedicated his life to chicken. As it turns out, most of his life seems to have been given to just about everything but chicken. More to the point, I think it is safe to say that the bulk of Harland David Sanders's life story was the tale of a man who never found his niche. His *curriculum vita* was a litany of various positions (railroad worker, lawyer, businessman, insurance salesman, motel owner), and none of them seemed to work out very well. When Sanders was fifty, he rebuilt a burned-down motel. Then when he was sixty-five, he learned that a new interstate would bypass his motel and bankruptcy seemed imminent. With one last idea in his head, Sanders decided as a desperate expedient to franchise the chicken he served there. The rest, of course, is history. When most adults would be getting ready to retire, Colonel Sanders was finally on track with his first successful career—so successful that his face would one day become an internationally recognized iconic image. Sometimes finding one's groove takes a while.

A Life in Thirds

So it was with Moses. The book of Acts, in Stephen's testimony before the Council, tells us that Moses spent the first forty years of his life in Pharaoh's court (Acts 7:23), the next forty years as a fugitive who got by as a desert-bound shepherd (Acts 7:30), and only the last forty or so years of his life leading what would become the greatest event in Israel's history. Granting the possibility that Stephen may have been using forty years as a round number, we can affirm that Moses' life can be evenly divided up into three phases or careers: Prince, Pariah (that is, outcast), and Prophet. Someone has said that Moses spent the first phase of his life thinking he was somebody, the next phase of his life realizing he was a nobody, and the final phase of his life learning what God can do with a nobody. This chapter will focus on the first two phases of Moses' life: his rise to princedom (when he thought he was somebody) and his fall to exile (when he discovered he was a nobody).

Our primary source for this life story is the biblical book of Exodus. We would be mistaken if we thought of the second book of the Bible as a kind of log, giving equal verbiage to roughly equal periods of time within Moses' life. The reality is that the bulk of Moses' life story comes to us as a highly compressed story. While Exodus 3–40 narrates a story that takes about sixteen months to unfold, Exodus 2, by contrast, covers a period of eighty years. Moreover, Exodus

2 tells a story that is very spare in detail with basically only three elements: Moses' birth, his interactions with several of his fellow Israelites and the murder of a fellow Egyptian, and his flight and marriage. These three events are conveyed not only for their biographical value and theological meaning, but also because of their foreshadowing elements in the final phase of Moses' career. Life has a way of repeating itself and coming full circle in ironic ways. So it was, as we shall see, with Moses.

Humble Heroes

In order to make sense of Moses' birth, we have to return to the rather daunting circumstances in which the Israelites had found themselves. Scripture records that Pharaoh's edict to enslave the Israelites did nothing to reduce their fertility. On the contrary, "the more they were oppressed, the more they multiplied and spread" (Exodus 1:12). As a result, the Egyptians came to fear and loathe the Israelites with increasing venom. This resulted in not only more fierce treatment of the Israelite slaves but also a new tactic to deal with the exploding alien population.

Pharaoh had devised a cunning plot involving, at least in theory, the collaboration of two Hebrew midwives. Although Scripture never provides the names of the Israelites' esteemed elders and doesn't even preserve the name of the Pharaoh (much to the dismay of modern scholars like myself who would be very interested to know just which Pharaoh we're dealing with here), it does give the names of these two women: Shiphrah and Puah. We would not be over-reading the text to surmise that the inclusion of their names, together with the omission of the names of other "more important" people like Pharaoh himself, was calculated to make a theological point. In the eyes of the God of Israel, the true heroes, the true movers and shakers, are not those who strive to make a name for themselves but the everyday, behind-the-scenes people who quietly make heroic efforts to honor God. In God's story in the Pentateuch, the names of the humble heroes of faith are immortalized. When over a thousand years later Jesus would say, "The first shall be last and the last first," he wasn't saying anything radically new.

Whether Shiphrah and Puah are the only midwives among the Israelites is unclear. Pharaoh's officials may have communicated to them as spokespersons for a larger, informal team of midwives that—much like a modern volunteer fire department—had come together to meet the community's needs. In part, this all depends on how we extrapolate the number of Israelites at the time. If their population was about ten thousand, then two midwives would seem to have been sufficient. In any case, given the note that Yahweh eventually gave both midwives families of their own (Exodus 1:21), we infer that both were married women who up until this point had experienced difficulty conceiving their own children. Their childless state may well also explain how they got to be midwives in the first place. (Just as a modern obstetrician needs to be ready to go 24/7, the same obviously went for the birthing experts of antiquity—a bit of a trick for a busy mother in an agrarian society.) Shiphrah and Puah must have been married long enough to allow for the deferred dream of children to shrivel but were not so old as to have reached menopause. We could probably surmise that they were thirty- or forty-somethings. Given that this was probably at the upper register of life expectancy and given their crucial role in perpetuating Israelite society, Shiphrah and Puah would have likely been regarded as leaders within the community.

Pharaoh had a plan and a corresponding set of instructions. He informed the Hebrew midwives of their duties as follows: "When you serve as midwives to the Hebrew women, and see them on the birth stool, if it is a boy, kill him; on the other hand, if it is a girl, let her live" (Exodus 1:16). It's not entirely clear just what Pharaoh was asking. When we read the word translated "birth stool," we must remember that the original Hebrew word (*ābnayîm*) may not necessarily mean "(stone) birth stool" at all. Weighing against this interpretation is the archaeological evidence that tends to show women of the period squatting or kneeling to give birth, not sitting on a stone stool. Another option is to suppose that *ābnayîm* means genitalia. On this theory, supported by a number of scholars, the proper translation would go something like this: "When you . . . look at the genitalia, if it is a boy, kill him." In my mind, this is a clear improvement on "when you see them on their stone birth stools."

Still, both of these explanations have a problem when we try to imagine just how all this was supposed to work. Let's just say that Pharaoh had instructed the midwives to kill the male newborns at birth, either as the midwives saw the Israelite mothers on the birth stool or after they had identified the gender of the baby by looking between the baby's legs. Here's my question: Just how were the midwives supposed to go about killing each newborn baby boy without the mother, much less other people in the room, noticing?

I remember very clearly the birth of my two sons. As soon as those babies were out of the womb, they gave very clear indications that they were very much alive. Now let's just imagine a post-delivery scenario for one of these boys different than the one I experienced. The baby is born, and I decide to slip away for a few minutes to go downstairs to the hospital cafeteria to see whether they are serving barbeque for lunch that day. (For all I know, that could be my last shot for a good eighteen years or so!) Then I return only to find my son, who moments ago was very much alive, dead. Do my wife and I then say to the presiding health care professional, "Gee, that's funny. Seemed like the baby was doing so well just a second ago. Oh, well. You win some; you lose some"? No, I imagine we would begin to ask questions, lots of questions. And, whether or not we are satisfied with the answers to those questions, we would still share widely the tragedy of how our son was born, breathing and crying and carrying on fine one minute but dead the next minute when our backs were turned.

Now put this back in the Israelite context, where news travels fast in such tight-knit communities. You can be sure that Shiphrah and Puah would come under considerable scrutiny the next time either of them walked in the door to help deliver a baby. Yes, the neo-natal mortality rate of ancient Egypt was very high, even perhaps between 30 percent and 50 percent; nevertheless, we have to imagine that such murderous midwives would not get very far. Even so, if they were sneaky enough to avoid being caught, the pregnant mothers of Israel would make sure to find someone *other* than Shiphrah and Puah to be their midwife. As a long-term plan for controlling Israel's population, this was unfeasible—so unfeasible for some critical scholars that it must be regarded as legendary.

But not so fast. In my view, we have yet another way to look at this, an approach that was suggested about ten years ago by Scott Morschauser. Morschauser argues that the word *'ābnayîm* here should be taken to mean "potter's wheel." As I write this, I have a card on my desk inviting my wife and me to a baby shower. The front of the card shows a stove with a small piece of bread inside; the text simply says: "Bun in the oven." We all know what that metaphorical expression means. In ancient Egypt, the analogous expression was "on the potter's wheel." Plugging this in for *'ābnayîm*, we can re-translate Exodus 1:16 with the following dynamic equivalent: "When you act as midwives to the Hebrew women, and see that they have a bun in the oven, if it is a boy, kill him." Although the ancient Egyptians did not have sonogram technology, we do have records of their medical texts which describe—with perhaps not as much scientific backing as we would like—exactly how one may determine the gender of a baby *in utero*. So then, if Pharaoh thought that a baby's gender could be determined well before delivery, we can imagine him asking the midwives to make this determination and then, at the time of delivery, perform a covert abortion during the labor stage so that it would appear as a natural stillbirth. Who would know otherwise?

As cunning as this plan might have been, it is thwarted by the women's determination to "fear God" (Exodus 1:17). They resisted by refusing to carry out Pharaoh's orders, even if that meant, as they well knew it could mean, the cost of their own lives. While we should not load too much theological content into the phrase "they feared God," I still think that this resistance gives us a random soil test of the Israelites' spiritual and ethical life. True, it would be anachronistic to think of the Israelites as having a scripture or any written code encapsulating what the God of Abraham, Isaac, and Jacob demanded. At the same time, judging by Yahweh's subsequent interactions with Israel, including the call of Moses (Exodus 4), we infer that the enslaved people had not only held on to their storied religious traditions but were also able to draw ethical implications from those traditions. Ancient Israelite religion was not strictly a family affair but was held in common by the clans and tribes. The people's shared faith impacted their lives, sometimes in remarkable ways.

Eventually, perhaps after some months, the failure of the scheme becomes all too obvious, even to Pharaoh. As one might expect, a disappointed Pharaoh calls a follow-up meeting with Shiphrah and Puah. While the ruler of Egypt probably hadn't busied himself directly with the earlier interview, this time he checks back personally by summoning the two women to his court. We can only imagine the anxious scene at the respective homes of Shiphrah and Puah: The Egyptian officers suddenly appearing, sternly announcing Pharaoh's summons, waiting as the midwives embraced their husbands perhaps for the last time. Shiphrah and Puah both had known all along that this moment would eventually come. They had been practicing their explanation, their "story," and had probably been internally rehearsing their lines for months.

So they appear in the king's court. Their story to Pharaoh, simply enough, is that Israelite women are "vigorous" or "active" and give birth before the midwives can arrive. This is, of course, a lie. But it is a lie that Pharaoh apparently believes as he lets the women go their way. Interestingly, God blesses that lie (Exodus 1:20–21). The Hebrew canon gives other instances in which God's faithful lie in order to save their own necks (David before Achish, 1 Samuel 27) or the necks of God's people (Rahab before her interrogators, Joshua 2). Sometimes, God's people find themselves in situations where they are confronted with two evils and must choose between the lesser of the two. Because life is sometimes messy, our responses to ethical dilemmas can sometimes feel just as messy, even if they are the right responses.

Into the River

But Pharaoh is not about to be denied. "All right then," we can almost hear him say, "if Plan A won't work, we can go with a Plan B, a plan which involves the whole nation of Egypt in enforcing it." The edict goes out: Now every newborn male is to be cast into the Nile. And, by the way, all those who consider themselves Egyptian citizens in good standing will be expected to share the policing effort.

Needless to say, the edict is evil and horrific. It was also impractical. Anyone who has ever held a newborn knows that it would not take too much force or ingenuity to bring that little life to an abrupt end. Surely Pharaoh could have simply ordered death for the Israelite male newborns by any practical means. Why then did he specifically stipulate death by drowning in the Nile? The short answer is that we don't know, but we can make some guesses. First of all, by Pharaoh requiring the Egyptians to throw the infants into the Nile, he could be sure that the river's currents would send the little bodies irretrievably downstream. To put this bluntly: Death by drowning in the Nile was cleaner than just about any other conceivable means—no blood, no body, no burial, no burial space. The infant would simply be gone. "Out of sight, out of mind, now get back to work!"—or so perhaps Pharaoh thought.

A second guess, not incompatible with the first, is that Pharaoh saw this as way of sacrificing to the god of the Nile (and the god of fertility as well as fish and birds), Hapi. According to the Egyptians, Hapi was responsible for the annual flooding of the Nile, which deposited valuable silt on the river banks. Since all of Egyptian life revolved around the Nile, and Hapi was the god of the Nile, Pharaoh's job description could have no more important item than to keep Hapi . . . well, happy. As a result, ironically, what was the god of life to the Egyptians became the god of death to the Israelites.

Into this exceedingly dark context, Moses was born. Clearly this context also posed challenges for Moses' parents, Amram and Jocabed, who had to devise their own plan for keeping the Egyptians in the dark about their newborn son. Initially, it was simply a matter of hiding the child. But after three months, perhaps as the infant's vocal chords were becoming too powerful, they were forced to develop a new strategy. As the story is classically told, Jocabed gives up all hope of saving her baby boy, and thus entrusts him to Providence by setting him adrift on the river. Personally, I am not convinced by this explanation, nor does the Hebrew text require it. Instead, I believe we have to imagine a different scenario.

Here's what happened. In order to put teeth on Pharaoh's new policy, the Egyptian police would have to organize their own regular sweep of the Israelite neighborhoods, one that moved door to door. These would be highly unpleasant visits, to say the least. We know that the Egyptian police were armed with long staffs, and we suppose that they would have forcefully and unhesitatingly applied those staffs to the Israelites if they sensed the least interference. Images and texts preserved from antiquity also indicate that they employed both a canine unit (trained dogs) and a cercopithecinae unit (trained monkeys). Even if you were innocent of harboring a newborn male, the regular intrusion and intimidation—not to mention the "creep factor" of those monkeys—would have been intolerable.

Meanwhile, the Israelites pulled together in an act of collective resistance. I imagine Amram and Jocabed's neighbors developing a coded signal system that alerted the newborn's mother to the approach of the Egyptian police. On receiving this signal, Jocabed would place her son in a papyrus-wrought chest (not a basket as so typically depicted), which had been coated with tar as an extra sealant and kept at the river bank among the reeds. Once the baby was in the chest and the chest in turn was put out in the water—far enough into the river to make the crying inaudible from the houses on the shore, yet close enough to remain hidden within the reeds—it fell to Moses' older sister to keep an eye on things. (While the sister is not named, this is probably our first introduction to Miriam, who would later play an important role.) If this sister was, say, between eight and fifteen years old, she would be old enough to "babysit" her little brother from a safe distance but not quite old enough to attract attention from the Egyptian officials. Obviously, this was a lot of work, but in a situation like this, a mother will make just about any personal sacrifice for her baby.

Just how frequently Moses' family would have been forced to undertake this rather nerve-racking exercise, we don't know. But if this is the way it happened, then every time the boy's family moved into action, shunting the baby out of the house and down to the river out of earshot, each conspiring family member must have been thinking on the inside: "Even if we fool them this time, how long can we really pull this off?" Surely, so they must have thought, it would only be a matter of time before the gig was up.

Providential Care

Then one day it happened. Pharaoh's daughter and her attendants come down to the Nile so that the princess could bathe. Perhaps this was no everyday bath. For everyday baths, Egyptian royalty would presumably have the servants fetch water and fill a private bathtub back at the palace. Given the circumstances, the princess may be engaging in a kind of ritual in order to win favor with Hapi, who we remember is the Nile-based god of fertility. One explanation for her doing this would be her own inability to conceive children. Now just as she is making supplications to the god of the Nile that she might one day have her own child, she hears a cry. Next she sees the floating chest and promptly sends her servant to retrieve it. When the chest is brought to her, she opens it up and sees what is inside. In a moment, she connects the dots and realizes that this is an Israelite baby boy. "Is it possible," she instantly wonders, "that this baby is the answer to my prayers for a child?"

Observing all this from a distance, Moses' sister senses the princess's gushing maternal instincts and is no doubt instantly relieved. Then, in a brilliant and bold move—especially for a girl of her age—she walks right into the midst of the royal retinue, approaches the princess directly, and offers to find a wet nurse. Of course the sister also knows exactly who that wet nurse would be. Remarkably, the princess agrees to the suggestion on the spot, and the girl is off running back to the house to fetch her mother, confident that the family's ongoing crisis of three months has now been, suddenly and unexpectedly and delightfully, resolved. By the end of the afternoon, the princess, in flat contravention of her father's decree, has hired Jocabed to nurse the three month old and sends mother, baby, and sister all back home to their own house. (The grammar of the Hebrew text implies as much.) If securing the little baby's life on the highest authority wasn't enough, Jocabed can now also look forward to being remunerated handsomely—royalty never do anything on the cheap—for breastfeeding her own baby. This was a miraculous day.

Just how much interaction the adoptive princess had with Moses in his earliest years, we do not know—probably minimal. At the same time, we can imagine that Moses' earliest memories were now forming in the midst of his Israelite family. Here he would bond with his mother (ancient Egyptian mothers would carry their children around with them in a sling up until about age three), his older sister Miriam, and his older brother Aaron. That he maintained these relationships through adulthood is all but certain, given subsequent events. Yet at the same time, the boy's parents knew that they had to prepare their son for life in Pharaoh's palace. If Miriam was already proficient both in her Semitic mother-tongue as well as in the (partially related) language of the Egyptians, as appears to be the case given her communication with Pharaoh's daughter, we expect that Jocabed and Amram did whatever they could to make sure that their boy knew the Egyptian language before heading off to the palace. Aside from the added emphasis on cross-cultural training up until the age of three or four (the typical age for weaning in ancient Egyptian culture), Moses would have been raised like any other Israelite child.

New Family, New Name

Finally, the day of transition came. And when it did, Pharaoh's daughter thought it appropriate to give the boy a new name: "When the boy grew up, she brought him to Pharaoh's daughter, and she took him as her own son. She named him Moses, 'for,' she said, 'I drew him out of the water'" (Exodus 2:10). The princess's choice of name shows respect not only for Moses' Israelite roots ("Moses" sounds like the Hebrew active participle *moshē*, meaning "one who draws"), but also for Egyptian tradition and culture, which is fraught with similar such names, Amen*mose*, Thut*mose*, Ra*mose*, etc. The name Moses itself was in this respect bi-cultural, foreshadowing

Moses' own identity as a man caught between his earliest roots and his adoptive roots.

While skeptical scholars have in the past pooh-poohed the historicity of Moses' rise to the pharaonic court basically as a story too good to be true, the historical facts corroborate the authenticity of the biblical account. Under the reign of Thutmose III (1457–1425 B.C.), the Egyptians of the New Kingdom initiated a practice whereby the children of international client kings would be brought to Egypt to learn from the best tutors of the land right in Pharaoh's court. The technical name for such a student was "child of the nursery." Thutmose III wisely reasoned that if tomorrow's best and brightest from around the world could come to Egypt in order to appreciate Egyptian language and culture from a young age, this would only strengthen Egypt's profile and standing in the future. Think of the Fulbright Scholarship Program that was designed to send U.S.-born scholars and other professionals all over the globe in order to foster multi-national understanding. Except with the Egyptian king's "nursery," the flow was to be centripetal rather than centrifugal. As any Egyptian official might put it, "It is more important that they get us than that we get them." The proven existence of international boarding schools right under Pharaoh's roof in the New Kingdom period fits perfectly the scene described in the Bible.

For Moses, school would have started around age five. He would have been expected to learn three types of written languages: an everyday cursive, hieroglyphics (roughly seven hundred signs), and a writing form that was something in between these two. Students would sit on the floor with their limestone palettes in cross-legged position, copying, reciting, and memorizing important texts. As any student would find out, actually learning this common core curriculum was very important. One bit of Egyptian pedagogical wisdom goes as follows: "A boy's ear is on his back. He listens when he is beaten." Obviously, you learned to pay close attention to your tutor, whether or not you were "a Pharaoh kid."

One story the young charges would undoubtedly learn from an early age was the *Tale of Sinuhe*. As the *Iliad* would come to serve the ancient Greeks, so the *Tale of Sinuhe* served the ancient Egyptians. It was one of those stories that the educated would know, handed down from generation to generation. In the narrative, an official named Sinuhe overhears a politically sensitive conversation that forces him to flee Egypt. During the escape from Egypt, he almost perishes from thirst in the desert, only to be rescued by desert nomads. Longing to return to his native Egypt, he prays to the gods that he might return to his homeland. Finally, he receives an invitation from the new king, welcoming him back home. He gladly accepts the invitation, lives happily ever after in Egypt, and of course—the life goal of every Egyptian—dies happily ever after, too. The point of the story, like the point of many stories told in Pharaoh's court, is that Egypt is the best country ever.

How young Moses squared this thinly veiled politico-religious propaganda with his parents' teaching, namely, that *their* god, the God of Israel, was the true Creator God, we shall never know. The conflict between the claims of Pharaoh's sophisticated tutors and the claims of Moses' own fairly unsophisticated parents must have caused no small amount of cognitive dissonance. Eventually, after a while, that dissonance would finally be resolved.

Murderous Confrontation

For whatever reason, the biblical story does not dwell on Moses' youth. We will never know whether or not Moses married while a young man in Egypt; we will never know what he did as a teenager—or for that matter what he did in his twenties and thirties. Instead, the narrative skips ahead to two incidents: one involving a murder; the other, a marriage. The story of the murder begins with Moses, now about age forty, going out to his people (literally the Hebrew reads, "his brothers") and simply observing their way of life, in particular, their burden of labor. (Although James Hoffmeier may be correct in supposing that Moses is here undertaking official administrative business.) Unless Pharaoh's daughter had managed to sequester Moses in the palace for four decades, this certainly was not his first exposure to the plight of his people. Obviously, as much as anyone can remember in the first three or four years of life, Moses recalled his very earliest years as one who lived in the midst of slavery.

In his recollections, Moses must have reflected on his transfer at a young age into Pharaoh's court with all its comforts and advantages. How he felt about his fellow Hebrews at age fifteen or age twenty-five or age thirty-five—again we will never know. Perhaps he cared deeply. Perhaps he was too self-involved and could hardly have cared less. The point is this, for whatever reason—call it a mid-life crisis involving a reevaluation of life goals and values—

Moses makes a conscious decision to be with his people. This is no detached, purely journalistic interest. The scriptural text leaves no room for such an interpretation. No, Moses is sensing the need to return to his roots and express solidarity with the very people who conspired to save him from the Egyptians.

Then it happened. One day, while brooding over the socio-economic plight of his kin, Moses notices an Egyptian beating a fellow Israelite. Next, in pre-mediated fashion, Moses follows the assaulter in the hopes of finding a good opportunity. The opportunity comes: The coast is clear, and he kills the slave beater in an act of vengeance. Next, moving hastily, he finds a mound of sand nearby (always in abundance in Egypt) and buries the corpse above ground. Wiping his hands clean, he leaves the scene and is on his way, seemingly undetected. In the end, he is confident that he has not only successfully served vigilante-style justice but also managed to get away with it.

He could not have been more wrong. Feeling his oats after dealing with that bullying Egyptian, Moses is out and about the next day, once again among "his brothers." As it so happens, he encounters yet another violent bullying situation, this time between two Hebrews. Apparently, one of the two was getting a clear upper hand because, as the story is told, Moses indignantly addresses only one of the men: "Why are you striking your companion?" The man in control of the street fight then stops but only long enough to respond to Moses in a deeply sarcastic and accusatory tone: "Who set you up as a ruler or judge over us? Will you be killing me as you killed the Egyptian?" (Exodus 2:14).

This is not the response Moses is counting on in two respects. First, Moses had grossly misjudged how his efforts to be helpful would be received. To grasp all this, we should picture the scene using our informed historical imaginations. If we can know anything, we can be sure of how Moses was dressed and groomed. (Ancient Egyptian fashion, much like Egyptian society in general, was extremely conservative in the sense that fashions simply did not change for centuries upon centuries.) Moses would be shirtless and wearing a linen *schenti* (skirt) wrapped around his hips, likely embroidered, perhaps with gold threads. Unlike Charlton Heston or Christian Bale, his head would be shaved completely bald or mostly bald (some men would sport a patch of long hair on the side); his eyes would be thickly accented with dark eyeliner. From his ears would dangle large, golden earrings; likewise, on his fingers, he would have been wearing plenty of ostentatious rings. Moses also probably smelled like a rose: Egyptian nobility, men and women alike, had a penchant for skin creams, deodorants, and perfumes. The street-fighter Israelite may also have been wearing a *schenti* (though in this case no embroidery and woven from course plant fibers), but that is about where the comparisons end. Moses looked like he had just walked out of a man makeover; the Israelite slave looked like he had just emerged from the sewer. Add to this visual a quick browbeating from this so-called Israelite, who has had a silver spoon firmly planted in his mouth since age three months, telling his "brother Israelite" slave how to handle his affairs and squabbles. Well, Moses' best intentions just didn't have a chance of going over well.

The second surprise for Moses was the outing of his dirty little secret from the day before. It was not only "outed," as he suddenly found out, but it apparently was a matter of common knowledge. Of course, this explains even more the bullying Israelite's indignation over Moses' role as Mr. Butt-in-ski. Consider again the scene step by step. Just imagine, as would be entirely plausible, that the Egyptian whom Moses murdered was an Egyptian foreman. When the foreman did not come home that night, his concerned wife contacted her husband's supervisor. Before long, the authorities do a sweep of the area, notice a pile of sand that wasn't there yesterday, poke around in the sand, and behold—the missing foreman, battered and bloodied. When an Egyptian foreman, perhaps known for beating on Israelite slaves, suddenly shows up as a murder victim, we can be pretty sure that there would be you-know-what to pay. And you-know-who would be the ones to pay.

While Moses may have thought he was doing "the brothers" a favor by killing the physically abusive Egyptian, in reality he actually could not have done them a bigger disservice. Of course, Moses may not have put that together, much less foreseen such unintended consequences of his action. But the Israelites—including the one whom Moses wants to referee in the street fight—would have understood it fully. Fortunately for the implicated Israelites, someone had in fact spotted Moses either in the act of beating the Egyptian or burying him. Once the witness went on record, an ancient Egyptian equivalent of an APB went out. Overnight, Moses, a prince of Egypt, tops the Most Wanted List. Ironically, the prince himself appears to be among the last to find out. Moses' spectacular rise into the charmed life as an infant is now only outdone by a mid-life meteoric fall from grace.

In this instant, Moses is no longer thinking about helping two street fighters settle their differences amicably; he is instead thinking about how to save his own skin. Whether he even took the risk of going back to the palace one last time to gather what he could, we will never know. Scripture informs us that Pharaoh learns of all this soon enough and is, from that point on, determined to have his adoptive grandson arrested and executed. Execution Egyptian-style was no picnic. In this case, the Pharaoh would have likely had his grandson publicly impaled on a sharpened, vertically upright stake—rectum first. Impalement was a slow gruesome death ultimately brought about by the weight of the victim's own writhing body. Needless to say, the idea of going back to Pharaoh and hoping for clemency would have been too great a risk for Moses.

At any rate, that would have been a completely unrealistic hope. For any ancient ruler, the act of publicly humiliating the royal household through this kind of news-story-turned-public-relations-debacle would have made the chances of pardon remote enough. But we must add to this fact that here Moses was dealing with the office of Pharaoh of Egypt. Essentially, the Pharaoh had one job and one job only: maintain *ma'at* in the land; that is, ensure the proper balance of civic order and harmony with an iron fist. Thus, to let slide an Israelite act of murderous vengeance against an Egyptian foreman would be a betrayal of Pharaoh's most sacred duty. For Moses to ask for forgiveness in this situation would be tantamount to asking Pharaoh to give up his throne. This was not about to happen.

Nor would Pharaoh have necessarily been conflicted about carrying out his judicial duty in respect to his adoptive grandson. While Hollywood may give us a more interesting storyline by suggesting that Moses was adopted into a small and tight-knit family under the close watch-care of Pharaoh himself, we have to recall that the supreme ruler of Egypt had not only many wives (most of them married to secure political alliances), but also, correspondingly, many children—and again many, many more grandchildren. (Rameses II, for example, had two hundred wives and over a hundred children.) So then, while Pharaoh had probably met Moses now and again as a boy or a young man, this would have presented no impediment to him. Business was business, and family—well, that was business, too.

The Desert Escape

So off Moses goes into the desert, into the land controlled by the Midianites. We are not exactly sure where Moses landed, and even historians slightly closer to our own time, like Josephus (first century A.D.) and Eusebius (third century A.D.), can't seem to agree either. Let's just say it was in the area east of the Sinai Peninsula, east of the Elanitic Gulf (the modern-day Gulf of Aqaba), the northwest corner of modern Saudi Arabia. The journey would have been a good three hundred miles—say, at least the distance between Chicago and St. Louis, a good two-week journey by foot or donkey, maybe more. (Camel riding would not be invented for another six to eight hundred years.) If you have ever driven on the interstate from Chicago to St. Louis, you know that the route has long stretches through barren flat land, alternating with more populated areas, complete with exits leading to motels and fast-food options. Moses' journey to Midian would have been somewhat similar. After following "the Way of Horus" along the coast, an international highway regularly marked by well-stocked rest stops for traveling caravans, Moses would have then had to cut south into the harsher desert. Here he would take routes prescribed by the locals. Accidentally get off the path or fail to find the hidden sources of water along the way, and you would be dead within a few days. We can only imagine that lines from the *Tale of Sinuhe* echoed in Moses' mind as he traveled.

Of course, one might fairly ask why Moses decided to go *so* far away. After all, this distance may seem like an extreme response— almost like a fugitive fleeing Albuquerque, New Mexico, in order to take up a new identity in the woods of New Hampshire. But the reality is that the Egyptian empire was far-flung. Not only did the Pharaohs of the New Kingdom have diplomatic ties with every important nation and empire in the known world, but the fingers of trade and industry reached pretty far as well. There is good historical evidence for this. For example, archaeologists have discovered the remains—contemporaneous with Moses—of a well-equipped, well-catered turquoise mining industry active at Serabit el-Khadem, a location in the desert-like west central Sinai Peninsula. Proto-Sinaitic inscriptions there also indicate the presence of resident workers from Canaan, worshippers of Baalat (the female analogue to Baal), and the god El. Here were folks who made regular treks back and forth to the Levant, also rubbing elbows with other folks who made regular trips to and from Egypt. For Moses, giving such people a lot of room would have been the better part of wisdom. If he wanted to be in a space where he could start a new life with minimum contact with Egyptians, he would have had to make an extra effort.

As for the Midianites, they controlled much of the northern Arabian Peninsula as well as the south Transjordan (southwest modern Jordan). They claimed Abraham as their father (Genesis 25:2); they also had the dubious distinction of serving as the middle-men when Joseph was sold as a slave to Egypt (Genesis 37:28). In this period, they seem to have been constituted by a powerful confederation of tribes, although in due course this would change dramatically when the Midianites are summarily dispatched in battle (Numbers 31). Perhaps ancient Jews saw this as payback for the Joseph thing.

The bulk of the Midianites, like the Kenites and Rechabites, took up metal-smithing. This profession entailed its own distinctive lifestyle, involving whole families moving about from village to village like traveling salespersons, offering to mine metal and forge everything from swords to mower blades. If like Reuel (also known by his honorific title "Jethro"), Moses' father-in-law, you served as a Midianite priest as an avocation, you might have your own cache of incense bowls and *masseboth* (pillars used in cultic veneration). Artifacts such as these have been found in the eleventh-century B.C. Midianite-layer remains at Serabit el-Khadem. Whatever Reuel's wage-paying profession, we can suppose Moses' newest adoptive family moved about in search of grazeable land for their flocks—no mean trick in a part of the world that gets an average of two-and-a-half inches of rain per year (half the amount of rain Chicago gets in

August alone). Theirs was an itinerant lifestyle, a fact that perhaps would help prepare Moses for one day leading Israel through their own itinerant experience.

Moses' hair and clothing may explain how Zipporah and her six sisters, all daughters of Reuel, recognized this strange traveler coming over the horizon as an Egyptian (cf. Exodus 2:19). Although the Midianites would have been considered backwoods by the Egyptians, they certainly would know an Egyptian when they saw one. Moses appears on the scene just as the young women are at an oasis watering their flocks. More exactly, they are trying to water their flocks when a band of shepherds attempts to force them to get out of the way for *their* flocks. Once again, Moses' keen sense of justice is violated: He comes to the girls' defense, waters their flock, and becomes their hero. Having taken Moses into the family, Reuel gives Zipporah's hand to Moses in marriage. In due course, Zipporah becomes pregnant and gives birth to Gershom. Another son by the name of Eliezer will eventually follow. Now with a wife and two boys, Moses is firmly ensconced in the land of the Midians.

New Identity, New Life

Moses the fugitive has created a new identity for himself. Once he was a prince in Egypt, a powerful man, widely recognized and feared. Now he is an anonymous shepherd, scratching out a desert existence wherever he can find the next source of water. Back in Egypt, Moses had been steeped in the richest culture and learning of the day. The land of the Midians had, by contrast, very little "culture" to speak of—only sand and rock. For Moses, life as a cosmopolitan

Egyptian prince must have seemed like another lifetime altogether, a way of life that neither Zipporah nor members of her family could even have categories for, much less understand. Of course, even if he were to return to Egypt (if the thought ever crossed his mind), how would he fit in? The Israelites would not treat him as one of their own, and neither would the Egyptians. Having spent the first forty years of his life as a third-culture kid (TCK); now, as a fourth-culture man, he is truly unable to claim any people as his own. At age forty, he is starting completely over: a new people, a new calling. Sometimes it takes a while to find your groove.

Midian is now his home away from home. Whatever religious life looked like in Egypt, whatever spread the Egyptian servants put out on the table—all this has changed. Now Zipporah involves her Israelite-Egyptian husband in the cultic life of her people. Now they are going to "Daddy's church," as it were. The fact that "Daddy" happens to be a Yahwist, much like Moses' parents, must have been the source of some comfort. Meanwhile, at the end of each day, Zipporah cooks Moses foods unique to the Midians. I wonder if he ever became attached to Midianite barbeque. And if he did, would he miss it when he learned he had to go back to Egypt?

PROPHET

ome on now. I will send you to Pharaoh so that you might bring my people, the children of Israel, out of Egypt." But Moses said to God, "Who am I that I should go to Pharaoh and bring the children of Israel out of Egypt?" He said, "I will be with you. And this will be a sign that it is I who sent you: once you have brought the people out of Egypt, you will serve God on this mountain." *(Exodus 3:10–12)*

Some days, life is filled with joy and thanksgiving. Other days are less filled. Then certain days nothing seems to go right. And on some of those days, if you're not careful, you may begin to feel yourself slide into a vortex of self-pity. I remember one of these days in particular. I was feeling as if God had called me to an impossible and intractable situation and, truth be told, I was angry about it. That evening, I decided to go outside by myself and vent before God.

Leaving the house, I went to a nearby park. Walking along the paved trail in the darkness, I found a park bench and sat down. Surveying the premises by the light of the moon, I saw that I was alone in the middle of a large field lined by distant trees. It was just me and God, and this was my chance to tell God how I was feeling.

Oddly, while I usually find that straight talk with God does my soul good, this was not my experience that particular night. In fact, the more I poured out my bitter disappointments, the more embittered I felt. Surges of deep doubt entered in. If God was doing such a bad job of managing my life, how could I really believe that he was Lord of the universe? Had the Lord really brought me this far to abandon me? The question I was struggling with at bottom was this: Will God be with me?

Suddenly in the midst of my park-bench crisis of faith, I heard a flapping noise followed almost immediately by the sensation of something sharp and powerful hitting me on the back of my head. In an instant, I leapt to my feet, took two or three quick strides forward, and then spun around on my heels to see what was happening. Looking back, I saw a large crow hovering over the bench and now backing off and returning to the distant trees from which it had presumably come. In an instant, I realized that, like a character in a scene from Alfred Hitchcock's *The Birds*, I had been attacked—attacked by a crow, of all creatures. Blame it on Edgar Allen Poe's poem "The Raven," but I have always found crows to be unpleasant and somewhat creepy. Now I had more reason than ever to be creeped out.

In any event, I felt as if someone had splashed cold water in my face. As far as I was concerned, the litany of questions and complaints was now officially over. Who knew? Maybe the crow was planning on a second dive-bomb or had simply gone back to the trees to get reinforcements. I wasn't about to wait around to find out. It was time to go. To this day I believe that God used an ordinary crow to get my attention in an extraordinary manner. God had spoken, and it was time to get on with my calling, ready or not. When your mind is set on your mission, you have no leftover space for self-pity.

Divine Irony

Something like this seems to have been the case with Moses' calling. Here the God of Israel gets Moses' attention by employing an ordinary bush in an extraordinary manner for an extraordinary mission. In some ways, that mission is God's rejoinder to Moses' well-meaning but ultimately misguided intentions when he killed the abusive Egyptian in the streets of Goshen. At that time, Moses had been interested in justice for Israel and had his own ideas about how to go about securing that justice. Now, years later, God is calling Moses back to the same basic causes—this time on God's terms.

Here is the irony: Now that God is finally ready to deliver his people, Moses is less than eager. In fact, he is downright reluctant. While we might expect Moses to jump at the chance, given his earlier heroics, we find the reverse. Pushing back against the one calling him from within the bush, Moses protests by citing his own inadequacies. While I am a historian and not a mind-reader, I sense that Moses' disinclination is partially borne of self-pity in regards to his exiled condition. Self-pity and passive aggressiveness (an unholy stubbornness) often go hand in hand.

Mountain of God

The scene begins at Mount Horeb. Despite the mountain's huge importance in the biblical story, today we are not completely certain of its location. But we have at least a good guess: Jebel Musa, toward the lower tip of the Sinai Peninsula. To get there, Moses must have come up to the top of the Gulf of Aqaba from the east and then back down south along its west coast and into the heart of the peninsula, all with Jethro's flocks in tow. Perhaps that year the land of the Midianites (northern Saudi Arabia) had been experiencing drought conditions that were forcing Moses to search far and wide for pasture. In any case, he was taking the livestock high up into the steppe, which means that the vegetation on the lower lands had been grazed over or wilted by the summer sun. (The annual shepherding season in that part of the world might be compared to eating a bowl of spaghetti: By the time you get to the end, you have to work harder and harder for every bite.) Moses had thought he had come a long way for the sake of his flock, but, in reality, he had come a long way for the sake of a different sort of flock altogether.

Although the biblical text names this landmark as "the mountain of God" (Exodus 3:1), the epithet was likely attached in retrospect. At the time of Moses' arrival (Exodus 2), nothing was distinctively Yahwehistic about Mount Horeb at all. On the contrary, good linguistic and archaeological evidence suggests that it served as the venue for moon worship. In fact, as Moses walked with his herd along the mountain base, he probably would have noticed on the ground broken bits of figurines or pottery dedicated to the moon god, Sin. At the same time, the mountain was hardly extraordinary, in terms of either religious significance or stature (coming in at an elevation of 7,500 feet, it is shorter than a good four dozen or so mountains in California alone). Yet this very ordinary mountain was about to become one of the most renowned mountains in the world, simply because the God of Israel had deigned to meet Moses there.

The Bush

The angel of the Lord, so the Scriptures inform us, appears to Moses in the form of a burning bush—a *sĕneh*, to be exact—a plant not much bigger than an eighteen-inch-high boxwood. To find an isolated burning bush in the desert without a human in sight would be very odd indeed. But what makes this sight not simply very odd but completely extraordinary is the fact that the bush, though burning, remains unconsumed. Needless to say, God now has Moses' full attention.

Of course a burning-yet-unconsumed bush is not only striking, it also constitutes a suspension of the so-called "laws of nature." While interpreters through the centuries have unhesitatingly granted the authenticity of this miracle and others like it in the Exodus narrative, many modern-day readers, philosophically committed to metaphysical naturalism, have balked at accepting this as a reliable history. Here, as is commonly assumed, we are moving squarely into the realm of myth or fairy tale. The line of such assumptive reasoning goes something like this: Although the Bible was written in a time when simple folk hardly batted an eyelid at miracles, we enlightened moderns know better; in this case, we know that no such thing as burning-yet-unconsumed bushes exist, much less, burning bushes that also talk! Therefore, so this thinking continues, it is nonsense to consider the account of the burning bush—or for that matter the plagues or the parting of the sea before Moses—as history.

The Miraculous

Since a number of miraculous events appear in the Exodus narrative, we need to respond to this interpretive grid by raising several objections to it. The scene of the burning bush makes for a good case study.

First, we must note here that the narrative of the burning bush conveys the event as being consistently real, giving no indication of shifting from fact to fantasy. In short, the text invites the reader to take the burning-yet-unconsumed bush at face value. At the same time, while the Bible obviously allows for the possibility of occurrences falling outside the bounds of ordinary human experience, we should not miss the fact that we are being invited to see the burning bush incident as an extraordinary event. Again, sometimes you'll hear people say, "Well, for those pre-Enlightenment ancients, such things as spirits, ghosts, and burning bushes were normal, and that's why we have this story here." But precisely because the biblical text never passes off this event as "normal" in any sense, this explanation simply doesn't work. On the contrary, Moses knows just as well as Stephen Hawking that bushes don't self-combust and that's exactly why—as the text makes clear—he is as puzzled as Hawking himself would be by this phenomenon. If burning-yet-unconsumed bushes were nothing for the "ignorant ancients" to write home about, then why would we have the story preserved in the first place? Maybe, just maybe, the very fact that the ancients didn't normally encounter such phenomena explains why we are still reading this story today.

At the same time, the burning bush scene is an event that demands a theological interpretation. This is what puts it in a slightly different category from my story of the Hitchcock-esque crow. Since crows are aggressive birds and have been known to dive-bomb people, my bird encounter *could* be fully explained without reference to God. But because a burning-yet-unconsumed bush defies scientific explanation, and also because God speaks from out of the bush, this amounts to—as much for Moses as for us—a revelatory act. (By the term "revelatory act," I mean a verbally interpreted divine in-breaking within the course of redemptive history that, as a word from God, either speaks to reality or brings into existence a new reality.) Some historians rule out ahead of time the possibility of a Creator God (a metaphysical, not a scientific, judgment call). Others allow for a Creator God but rule out the possibility of subsequent divine intervention (also a metaphysical decision). The Bible, however, takes a more expansive view that allows for both divine creation and divine intervention. Curiously, while naturalists or philosophical materialists will often claim the higher ground by playing the *scientific* trump card, a closer examination reveals that these same philosophical materialists fail to realize how they are invested in a supposedly scientific interpretation of reality that actually prejudges the nature of that reality on non-scientific grounds. Here is a certain irony: Although philosophical materialists will also often claim to be open-minded while accusing Bible-believing Christians of being "close-minded fundamentalists," the charge could actually be reversed. I suppose all this goes to show you that fundamentalism comes in all kinds of varieties, religious and secular.

The Fire

So much can be said about the burning bush, but I will focus on one point in particular: namely, the essential continuity between this event and the subsequent development of Israel's temple cultus.

This continuity comes to surface in several ways. First, the combination of fire and bush (*sĕneh*) here anticipates Moses' return to the same mountain when it will be called Sinai (*sināy*) and covered with fire. Throughout the biblical tradition, God employs fire as a kind of divine calling card (Genesis 15:17; Exodus 13:21; 19:18; Deuteronomy 4:24; 1 Kings 19:6; Psalm 50:3; Daniel 7:9; and more). Where one finds divine fire, one finds the presence of God. And where we find the presence of God, we will find sacred space (think, for example, of the pillar cloud of fire that entered Solomon's temple, 1 Kings 8:10–11).

That is exactly why God instructs Moses to remove his sandals, for he is standing on "holy ground" (Exodus 3:5). Again, God's insistence that Moses be shoeless in the sacred space stands in continuity with later Jewish practice. When later portions of Exodus (chapters 28 and 39) take up the topic of the priests' vestments, every article of clothing is covered in detail—every article, that is, except for footwear. The reason for this, we suppose, is because the priests knew that when entering God's presence, woe to them if they entered with anything other than clean, *bare* feet. Many centuries later, the same line of thinking would undergird Jesus' startling decision to wash the disciples' feet in John 13. As the evangelist sets it up, Jesus is essentially preparing his priest-like disciples to enter the holy space of the Cross. To this day in Middle Eastern culture, feet are regarded as ignoble parts of the body; shoes are downright impure. If you don't believe me, try wearing your Nikes into any mosque today and see how that works out for you.

Well after the Exodus and the giving of the law, Moses' vision of the burning bush would still remain emblazoned in his memory, especially when it came to designing certain paraphernalia utilized for the tabernacle. When Moses says to himself, "I need to turn aside and see this great *sight (mar'eh)*" (Exodus 3:3), this anticipates God's instructions to Moses to make the tabernacle's lampstand according to the *sight (mar'eh)* shown on the mountain (Exodus 25:40). After the image of the bush, the lampstand was to be cast with branches and blossoms; after the image of the fire within the bush, the lampstand was to burn continually (Exodus 27:20–21). The menorah of the second temple, a depiction of which can be seen today on the Arch of Titus in Rome (a first-century A.D. monument that was inspired by the Romans' plundering of Jerusalem and its temple in A.D. 70), traces itself all the way back to Moses' unexpected encounter at Horeb. Just think: The story of this menorah, which, together with the Star of David, endures as a familiar symbol of Judaism to this day, begins with Moses' unexpected encounter with God—on a day when his highest aspiration had been simply to find pasture for his sheep.

The Divine Plan

Having established this meeting as a holy transaction, God next reveals his intention to deliver the Israelites from under the hand of the Egyptians and bring them into the land of Canaan, a land flowing with milk and honey. We should not press this as a geographically accurate description. The point is not that Canaan is the most fertile tract of land in the world (it is not), but that it is relatively fertile compared to other regions within that part of the world. Still, it proved to be a good land for herding (goats' milk) and keeping bees (honey). By calling the area a "land flowing with milk and honey," God was simply saying, "You will be more than satisfied there."

The surprising news for Moses is that God expects the fugitive prince (of all people) to be the agent through which all of this will take place. For Moses, not only is the news surprising, it is also unwelcome. Despite the powerful way in which the God of Israel encountered Moses at Horeb, the very man he names as his prophet of choice has no interest in the job. He asks, "Who am I?" (Exodus 3:11)—in other words, "Who, me?!" As far as saving his fellow Hebrews is concerned, Moses has already mentally closed the book on that chapter of his life: "Been there, done it, got the T-shirt" and, oh, yes, "It didn't work out so well." What follows is a fascinating interchange in which Moses offers various reasons as to why someone—anyone—except him would be more suited to carry this prophetic mantle.

The Name

One particularly intriguing moment in this interchange is when Moses asks about the name of the God of Israel (Exodus 3:13). Moses' request is driven not so much by personal curiosity but by the perceived necessity of his being equipped with an answer should the Israelites ask him whether he did indeed encounter the God of the patriarchs ("Who did you say sent you?"). This makes sense. One can well imagine a number of Israelites arching their eyebrows at a Hebrew-turned-Egyptian, of dubious religious pedigree, who has come back to be their proverbial knight in shining armor. They might very well want to know the basis for Moses' claim to have met the God of the patriarchs. In this sense, Moses is looking for a kind of password that will corroborate his prophetic calling.

God's response to Moses is as famous as it is enigmatic: "I AM WHO I AM" (Exodus 3:14). That is the way in which the majority of English translations, perhaps decisively influenced by the wording of the King James Version, render it. This is not, however, by any means the only way to parse the Hebrew. In fact a good dozen or so possibilities exist, all involving the verb "to be" (*hyh*). Of these I have been personally persuaded by the translation: "I WILL BE WHO I WILL BE" (which happens to be Luther's reading continuing down to the 1984 *Luther Bibel*). Some scholars see God's response to Moses as a coy way of evading the question. But the very fact that God's answer, the tetragrammaton YHWH ("he who is"), is identified throughout Scripture with the God of Israel militates against this possibility. By self-identifying as *existence itself* (the Greek Old Testament, the Septuagint, here translates the Hebrew simply as "the Being"), the God of Israel insists on his own timelessness and limitlessness. As John Goldingay remarks, if Moses was looking for a label or category along the lines of the gods he knew in Egypt, the God of Israel responds by issuing a *theology*. None of this would be lost with the advent of Christianity, for God remains the one "who is and was and is to come" (Revelation 1:4), even as Jesus identifies himself as the I AM (John 8:58).

The Snake

Moses is still not satisfied. He still has concerns. Thinking ahead to what God is calling him to do, he raises a very practical question: What if the Israelites don't believe that Yahweh has appeared to him (Exodus 4:1)? In response to this query, Yahweh offers three signs, each of which might prove useful in persuading doubters of Moses' prophetic credentials.

In order to confirm the first sign, Yahweh instructs Moses to take his staff and throw it down to the ground. Moses obeys, and instantly the staff turns into a snake. As far as we know, the snake is ordinary, but it assuredly spooks Moses.

Next, Yahweh instructs the now-startled Moses to pick up the snake by the tail (no small request and not the safest way to pick up a snake). Moses dutifully complies and the writhing snake, once in his grasp, suddenly stiffens back into a staff. The sign is more than impressive and will later serve Moses well as he attempts to convince both his own people (Exodus 4:30–31) and Pharaoh's court (Exodus 7:8–13) of the divine backing of his cause.

This sign is altogether appropriate since it speaks to the Israelites (given their understanding of the redemptive story) as well as to the Egyptians (given their understanding of magic). While a number of commentators see no connection between Moses' serpent and the serpent of Eden (Genesis 3), I demur. When we think about the cycle of stories in Genesis, we begin with a story of temptation, prompted by the serpent, and sin. Yet even in Genesis, sin and death do not receive the final word. Instead, Yahweh calls Abra(ha)m in his determination to bless creation and its inhabitants (Genesis 12:1–3); it is a call issued in direct response to the unraveling of the created order through the sin of Adam and Adam's progeny. While Yahweh had given life to creation and all that is in it (including the serpent), the same God also promises, metaphorically speaking, to grab the serpent by the tail and render it as stiff and immobile as a wooden stick. In other words, the act of turning a wooden staff into a living snake is akin to the act of creation itself; the act of bringing the same fearsome serpent under control is analogous to redemption. Thus, in a highly symbolic manner, Moses presages his own role both as the one who would grant new life to Israel and as the one who would check the forces of serpent-inspired chaos, not least through the establishment of God's Kingdom on earth.

For the Egyptians, the snake represents the mysterious and potentially hostile forces of nature that, with any luck, could only be overcome through magical incantations. At the same time, control over such creatures was associated with a blessed post-mortem state or god-like status. For example, one spell within the Coffin Texts reads: "The snake is in my hand and cannot bite me." Likewise, if you ever go to the Egyptian Museum in Milan, Italy, you can see for yourself the fifth-century B.C. stele of Horus on the Crocodiles. On the stele, an image depicts the god Horus's feet firmly standing on two crocodiles, his hands securely grasping two serpents (symbols of Seth, the god of chaos) by their tails. While to modern Western readers of Exodus the act of retrieving a serpent by the tail seems little more than an impressive trick, the same action would have demonstrated personal power to subdue and harness the dark powers.

The Hand

After providing the first sign, Yahweh now offers a second sign as a backup plan. Accordingly, Yahweh instructs Moses to place his hand inside the fold of his garment. When Moses withdraws his hand from his cloak, it is leprous, "like snow" (Exodus 4:6). On re-inserting and re-withdrawing his hand, again at Yahweh's command, the hand is restored from its leprous condition. Here the biblical text is probably not intending leprosy as most of us today understand it (Hansen's Disease). Rather, given the Hebrew vocabulary, the condition of Moses' hand was probably a form of psoriasis or other skin ailment that entailed the flaking of the skin "like snow." This sign is not only a convincing indication that Yahweh has instant control over sickness and health (skin diseases are, by their nature, gradually developing ailments); it is also a symbolic expression of Yahweh's place to distinguish the pure from the impure. In later levitical law, "leprosy" constituted impurity and effectively put one outside the camp of Israel, even as it would in the case of Miriam, at least for a time (Numbers 12).

The River and Blood

The third sign granted to Moses is the ability to turn the Nile's waters into blood simply by pouring it onto the ground. In this case, differently from the first two signs, Moses is not given the ability to reverse the action. This third sign is also unique in that it is not used to convince the Israelites. It is saved rather for the Egyptians' benefit when Moses unleashes the first of the ten plagues against Egypt (Exodus 7:14–24). Yet it is a sign with a pre-history, at least in the world of Egyptian fiction. For instance, in the *Tale of Ipu-wer*, a text from the First Intermediate Period (2181–2040 B.C.), we have a similar allusion to the Nile turning to blood. Closer to the time of Moses, we find a tradition dateable to the reign of Rameses II

(1279–1212 B.C.) where a magician expresses his fear that if he loses the magical context in which he is engaged, the Nile will turn to blood. Given the Nile's importance to Egyptian agriculture and daily life, such an event, if actualized, would have been a natural disaster of epic proportions.

The symbolic significance of Moses pouring out the Nile water onto the ground, only to see it turn blood red, would have been manifold. First of all, Nile water and blood would have had very different connotations for the Israelites and the Egyptians. While the Israelites associated the Nile with the death warrant signed by Pharaoh himself for their firstborn males, the Egyptians saw the Nile as the ultimate giver of life. Conversely, Hebrew tradition tended to regard life as being bound up in blood (Leviticus 17:11, 14; Deuteronomy 12:23), where the Egyptian word for both "blood" and even the identical word "red" (*drsh*) was regarded as having evil connotations. This is evident, for example, in the fact that Seth, the Egyptian god of chaos, is typically depicted in a bold red. Given these two contrasting symbolic matrices between the two cultures, the act of transforming fresh Nile water into blood was meant to signify the victory of life for Israel even at the cost of Egypt's death. The sign was a kind of poetic justice for what the Egyptians had done to the infant boys who had not been as fortunate as Moses.

We should also note that the act of pouring liquid on the ground was a regular part of an ancient Egyptian funeral service. It symbolized the pouring out of human life and the returning of this life to the underworld. By engaging in the same act as Egypt's funerary priests (who were literally called "water pourers"), Moses would be symbolizing his own potential role, as it were, as Egypt's national funeral director. If the first two signs served to authenticate Yahweh's power over natural forces (including the demonic) and physical well-being, the third sign symbolically conveyed pure and irreversible judgment.

The Speaker

Notwithstanding these powerful portents, Moses remains resistant to Yahweh's call and appeals to his own inability as a public speaker (Exodus 4:10). Interestingly, Stephen's sermon in the book of Acts, which includes a good deal of the Moses story, says just the opposite, namely, that Moses "was powerful in words and works" (Acts 7:22). How are we to square these two apparently contradictory data? A couple of options are worth considering.

First, Moses may be a fully competent speaker but is simply just reaching for any excuse he can find to worm his way out of the trajectory being proposed by the angel of the Lord. Combining this possibility with the Middle Eastern predilection for overstatement (which continues down to this day), this becomes a sufficient explanation.

A second possibility is that Moses is a powerful speaker in one or two languages but foresees a steep learning curve in speaking to the Israelites in their native Hebrew language. True, Hebrew was Moses' mother tongue, but he most certainly fell out of practice with it after years in Pharaoh's court, where Hebrew was almost never heard, and among the Midians, who would have spoken but a cognate dialect.

A third option is that Moses has a kind of speech impediment, an interpretation supported both by rabbinic witness and the Septuagint; the latter describes Moses at Exodus 4:10 as stammering (*ischnophōnos*) and slow of tongue (*bradyglōssos*). A number of biblical commentators have ruled out this possibility, if not on the basis of Acts 7:22, then on the grounds of Moses' subsequent proven proficiency as a public speaker. Unlike these commentators, however, I am entirely prepared to believe that Moses had struggled with a speech impediment but nonetheless proved to be an effective public speaker over time. In this connection, we can think of well-known stammerers, from Demosthenes to Winston Churchill, who worked hard to overcome their disability to become some of the most notable orators in history. Perhaps the same God who was able to turn a piece of wood into an agile snake could do the same thing with a man's ineffectual tongue.

The Return

At the close of this longer interchange (with more excuses and finally Moses' plea, "Please send someone else"—Exodus 4:13), Moses eventually accepts the calling of God. He goes home with the sheep, asks his father-in-law's permission to return to Egypt, and then packs up his family for the move. God informs Moses that the Pharaoh who had sought his life is now dead. The door is open for Moses to return, and this time not to play the hero on his own strength but to serve Yahweh by leading the children of Israel. God had succeeded in getting Moses' attention; now it is time to go.

So Moses sets off with staff in hand. But now it is no longer just an ordinary staff, nor is it really Moses' private staff. For from here on out he will be required to share it with Yahweh, yielding it up to Yahweh's purposes. As the reluctant prophet anticipates the end of his journey, he must be picturing in his mind's eye meeting his long-lost brother Aaron, then the elders of Israel, and then finally Pharaoh himself. All three of these anticipated encounters must be anxiety-producing in their own way. Of this we can be almost certain: For every two steps forward Moses takes toward Egypt, he would much prefer taking three steps back. But God has spoken, and it is time to get on with the prophetic calling—ready or not.

PHARAOH

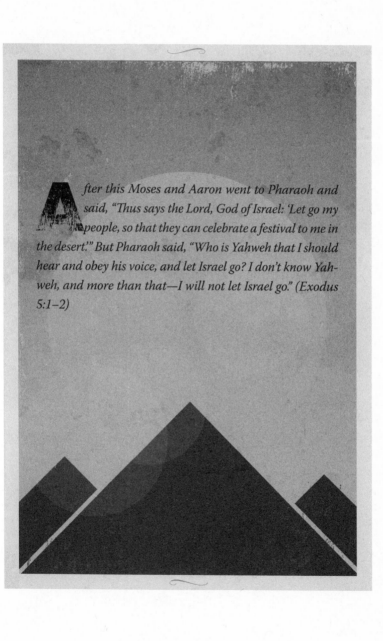

After this Moses and Aaron went to Pharaoh and said, "Thus says the Lord, God of Israel: 'Let go my people, so that they can celebrate a festival to me in the desert.'" But Pharaoh said, "Who is Yahweh that I should hear and obey his voice, and let Israel go? I don't know Yahweh, and more than that—I will not let Israel go." (Exodus 5:1–2)

Political confrontation can take all forms. Consider, for instance, the situation of a fifteen year old named Justina Pelletier. Justina's story began when administrators at Boston Children's Hospital called into question the diagnosis of her illness offered by a doctor at nearby Tufts Medical Center as a rare cell disorder. The second opinion, instead, theorized a psychosomatic illness as the underlying cause. Boston Children's Hospital then lodged charges of medical child abuse against Justina's mother and father. Very quickly, the teenager was removed from the custody of her parents who, in response, took up legal action against the hospital and the Commonwealth of Massachusetts. Eventually, a judge reviewed the case and ruled in favor of the hospital's decision.

By the time full custody of the teen had been awarded to the Department of Children and Family Services, however, Justina's case had already become a national *cause célèbre*, sparking impassioned responses from supporters of both "the system," on the one side, and Justina's parents, on the other side. Among the latter category, some no doubt decried the actions of Massachusetts out of sympathy for the family, others out of indignation over what was perceived to be quasi-totalitarian overreach; still others, a bit of both.

Rightly or wrongly, objectors to Justina's enforced separation issued from a wide variety of circles: from left-wing social libertarians to right-wing social conservatives, from underground cyber terrorists to well-respected op-ed columnists, and from state congressional leaders to leaders of national not-for-profit organizations.

Of course, a good deal of interchange on this issue was carried on the web. One might cite, for example, an Internet video that shows the director of the Washington-based Christian Defense Coalition confronting the governor of Massachusetts with the words: "You don't have a reunification plan. She cannot walk. She's not being educated. She wasn't allowed to go to church, sir . . . let's get her home." Through sound bites like these, as well as petitions and on-line pleas to make phone calls, the national effort to bring Justina home may one day prove to be a case study in the formation of a grassroots political pressure group. In a free and democratic society, popular-level dissent can be a powerful force.

Similar to Justina's parents, Moses was hoping to persuade "the system" to reconsider its policy. But unlike Justina's parents, he did not have the advantages of either the Internet or the American political system. Egypt under the Pharaohs was neither free nor democratic (nor online!). As Moses contemplated his strategy while traversing the desert sands back toward Egypt, he knew that the deck was stacked squarely against him. In short, he knew that Pharaoh was the absolute ruler with absolute power. Appealing to public support was not an option. While in modern Western society, public expressions of political dissent are common, in ancient Egypt such expressions did not even exist. They could not exist. What Pharaoh said happened. End of story.

Moses also knew from his growing-up years that giving in to requests for leniency or "looking soft" was almost never in Pharaoh's interest. Because each successive Pharaoh had to be ever watchful for a potential coup—more often than not brewing from within one's own palace—to show himself as a fierce and unbending ruler was conventional political wisdom for Egypt's king. For the Egyptians, making concessions was not a sign of compassion or fair-mindedness, but of weakness. As for human rights—well, the concept wasn't even close to being invented yet. At the end of the day, between Moses and Aaron, we have little more than two ethnically-other octogenarians who, having *almost* nothing in the way of social standing or political connections, would be seeking to win Pharaoh over to a cause that could only undermine his reputation and political power. By any human reckoning, the prospect of this Pharaoh or any Pharaoh releasing the Israelites in response to Moses and Aaron's overture was at best grim and at worst downright laughable.

It was almost as if Yahweh had asked Moses to move a mountain, and to do so with absolutely no palpable leverage. No palpable leverage—true enough. But he had leverage of another sort: the promise and the power of Yahweh, the God of Israel. Moses had nothing else to go on. As the writer of Hebrews reminds us (11:24–27), only by sheer faith did Moses make his way back to Egypt in order to see Pharaoh.

Why Aaron?

Before going to Pharaoh, Moses had a stop or two along the way. First, he would see Aaron, his older brother by three years. According to the biblical text, Yahweh had also spoken to Aaron and prompted him to meet Moses at Horeb (Exodus 4:27); it was a mini family reunion event, which, when we think about it, would have necessarily involved divine coordination of not only the specific place but also a window of time. Exactly how Aaron, a member of a slave community, was able to leave Egypt is left unexplained. Perhaps he escaped. Perhaps, as a man advanced in years, he was relieved of the kinds of daily labors to which his younger fellow Israelites would have been subject. That the rendezvous should occur at Horeb, not quite on the way, also seems to have been significant. I wonder: Was it important, from Yahweh's point of view, that the same redemptive mission that would culminate at Sinai should also begin at Sinai? If so, then the Exodus did not really start in Egypt. The Exodus started (and ended) here, at the mountain of God.

In retrospect, we can see why a forged partnership between Moses and Aaron would be crucial. First, we have to recall that to the degree to which the Israelites would remember Moses at all, they would remember him as an outsider. He would have been regarded not as an Egyptian but, worse, as an Israelite who had sold out to Egyptian ways. For this reason, it would take no less a person than Aaron, broadly respected within the community, to bridge the way for Moses.

In the first instance, Aaron's status as an eighty-three year old, a rare demographic in those days, would have earned him the floor in a culture that honored the wisdom of its seniors. In the second instance, given the way in which Aaron is able to pull together the elders of the tribe on demand (Exodus 4:29), we see that well before retrieving Moses from Midian, he already has a high level of social capital. Here we might draw an analogy with Barnabas who played the go-between for Saul, a.k.a. the Apostle Paul. When Saul, the persecutor-turned-apostle, had to meet Christians in Jerusalem for the very first time, a trusted mediator like Barnabas was needed to help smooth the way (Acts 9:26–27). As important as Moses was to the Exodus, in the beginning Aaron was even more important.

Why Moses?

If Aaron's role makes sense on the face of it, the same sense of "Aha, I get it" does not necessarily apply to Moses' calling. In fact, one might fairly ask, "Why Moses of all people? Why did God choose *him* to lead the Exodus?"

In some ways, such questions remain inscrutable, just as any question dealing with God's elective purposes is ultimately beyond our pay grade. Yet at the same time, we can see why Yahweh's choice of Moses, despite his status as an outsider, makes excellent sense. Think about it. On learning of the death of the old Pharaoh (the one who sought to take his life), Moses could have made a go of returning to Egypt and resuming his life at the palace, where surely at least a few old friends could put in a good word for him. Therefore, in choosing to forego a quiet retirement sipping umbrella-drinks by the royal swimming pool in order to pursue a very different course of leading the Israelites out of bondage, Moses is obviously sacrificing his own self-interests. On the face of it, a leader who comes into leadership this way will naturally have far more street-credibility than some ambitious Hebrew upstart with little to lose and just about everything to gain in appointing himself to the task.

Also, Moses' role is strategic, indeed critical, in another very practical respect: Apart from Moses' pull as a former palace resident, I seriously doubt that Aaron or any Israelite could have managed to secure a spot on Pharaoh's appointment calendar. (When we read the Exodus account, we might suppose that Moses and Aaron blithely walked right past the receptionist and into Pharaoh's office at will, but this was hardly the case.) Yes, just as much as Moses needed Aaron; Aaron, and indeed all the Israelites with him, also needed someone like Moses. In fact, someone *exactly* like Moses with his unique qualifications.

The Presentation

After Aaron and Moses assemble the elders, Aaron performs at least two of the signs that Yahweh had provided Moses. Whether he performs these signs in the presence of a small collection of elders representing the people or a much larger crowd constituting a critical mass of the people, the signs persuade the rank and file: "The people believed." And on hearing of Yahweh's concern for their plight, they respond by falling to their faces in worship. Whatever the depth of Israelite spirituality prior to this moment, when the Israelites heard the news that their God was about to deliver them from bondage, they responded in a spontaneous expression of awe and gratitude (Exodus 4:29–31).

In this, the very first recorded act of corporate worship in the Bible, we might perhaps find a lesson for ourselves. More exactly, we might pay attention to the nature of this worship. Sadly, many Christians today will evaluate their worship in strictly subjective terms, by the criterion of whether "I got anything out of the worship" on an emotional or sentimental level. In the biblical worldview, by contrast, worship is not so much a subjective experience occurring within the individual as much as an *inter*subjective response—occurring in, among, and between God's people—to what God has done or promised to do on behalf of his people. If so much contemporary worship involves our beating an inward retreat, ancient Israelite worship sets the bar by calling us to get outside of ourselves and respond to a God who has done something big.

The Challenge

Moses' next step would be gaining an audience with Pharaoh himself. This must have been a daunting challenge requiring, despite Moses' connections, weeks if not months of waiting after the initial inquiry. None of this would have come as a surprise to Moses, for he knew as well as anyone that the Pharaoh of Egypt was literally one of the most inaccessible people in the world. After all, the Pharaoh held the highest office in one of the greatest empires of the world.

Exactly how Pharaoh may have personally contributed to the smooth running of that empire would of course have varied somewhat from ruler to ruler. But at the same time, I think ancient Egypt's political traditions had a remarkable consistency, including a clearly proscribed vision of Pharaoh's responsibilities. Accordingly, for anyone acceding to the office of Pharaoh, life had a certain day-to-day predictability.

Whereas we do not necessarily have detailed knowledge of the king's daily activities in Moses' time, we may get some sense of the pharaonic rhythms from the report of the first-century B.C. Greek historian, Diodorus. According to Diodorus, the Egyptian ruler of the period began the day, like many of us begin our day, by answering (e)mail. Then, after the morning bath—here's where his day begins to look very different—his servants would dress him in his royal garments. Next, he might take a short walk from his private residence to the palace temple where the high priest would be waiting, ready to entreat the gods that they might bless Egypt's high ruler. While at the temple, the Pharaoh would listen to a priestly lector read from the sacred books and/or from the annals of history, not the least being biographical accounts of inspirational exploits of some great historical figure. Finally, no morning regimen would be complete without his assisting the high priest in offering the daily sacrifice to the gods. The remainder of the day would be given over to administration, holding audience for various appointments, taking meals, and allowing times for exercise and relaxation. Every detail of the day was accounted for and well planned—all the way down to Pharaoh's menu, which had been carefully proscribed by the court physician. As with modern royalty today, almost nothing was left to chance and everything had its own protocol.

Even if Diodorus's first-century B.C. account of "a day in the life of Pharaoh" is only roughly similar to the practices of Moses' period—that is, the New Kingdom (c. 1550–1070 B.C.)—notice that the

Pharaoh was expected to spend a sizable portion of his day in cultic activity. But this is entirely in keeping with what we would expect. As I have already hinted, the Pharaoh's first job was to be Egypt's chief chaplain, while his second job was to be Egypt's CEO. As important as administering the empire effectively was, an even more important responsibility was working with the gods. Pharaoh was seen as the son of Ra, the sun god; he alone was the appointed human receptacle for Ra's earthly existence. As such, it fell to Pharaoh to champion Ra and to give glory to the gods of Egypt as the true and highest deities. Keep the gods happy, and the rest was icing on the cake.

With this context in place, we are now in a better position to appreciate the difficulty of the challenge facing Aaron and Moses, who are about to ask Ra's chief representative to defer to the God of Israel.

The Reception

Now imagine Moses and Aaron on the day of the long-awaited appointment as they make their way through the bustling streets to the palace. Though Moses may well be tempted to reminisce as he walks past all the old familiar haunts, this is no time for nostalgia. Instead, as the two brothers draw closer and closer to the palace, we can imagine Moses hurriedly taking a last-minute opportunity to coach his older but less-experienced brother in what to expect, as well as in some of the "dos and don'ts" in meeting with royalty.

At last, Moses and Aaron arrive. There they tell the guards who they are and the nature of their business; of course, they are expected. From there, they are solemnly led from the palace entrance to an antechamber deep within the massive structure, a room adjacent to the *usechet* ("the wide") where Pharaoh, his courtiers, and his retainers would receive visitors. When finally Moses and Aaron are summoned, the doors open wide and they are ushered into the presence of the great king.

Even for Moses, a man well-experienced in palace life, the sight must have been impressive. The Pharaoh would have been sitting on a resplendent gold-plated throne ensconced within a large canopied structure, also covered in gold, marked off at each corner by four delicately carved wooden pillars: the Throne of the Living One or the Great Seat of Horus. If this throne was anything like that of the fourteenth-century B.C. King Tutankhamun (King Tut), then the top tier of the canopy would have been adorned with multiple graven images of the Uraeus (an upright cobra commonly associated with Pharaoh), which was symbolic of the ruler's sovereign power. At the base would have been recurring depictions of the legendary griffin (part lion and part eagle), symbolic of divine wisdom. Also engraved at the base of the throne, alongside the griffin and directly under the king's feet, would have been the countless rows of names of Pharaoh's defeated enemies from around the world. The symbolism of this roster of international *Who's Who* (or more exactly a *Who Used to Be Who*) situated beneath Pharaoh's feet would have been obvious enough!

The throne would have been surrounded by various royal courtiers, hierarchically positioned at different stations on a brilliantly colored carpet. To the immediate right and left would have stood the fan bearers, including not only those charged with keeping the king cool but also the flower holders who made sure that the wafting air was sufficiently sweet for the royal nostrils. (The title of "fan-bearer on the right" was actually a much-coveted high position within the court, even if the actual fanning was delegated to nearby servants.) Other counselors also would have stood there, in order of rank. Here gathered together in one room would have been the nerve center of the Egyptian empire.

And in the middle of it all would have been the Pharaoh himself, resplendently clothed in shimmering gold-pleated garments. His hands would have held the symbolic insignia of his rule: a crook in one hand, perhaps a whip or sword in the other. Unless donning a war helmet (not atypical headwear for Egyptian rulers of the New Kingdom), Pharaoh would have had his head covered with a long cylindrical crown with two long decorative folds hanging down past the ears and over the shoulders. Like any Egyptian noble, he would have been clean shaven, both head and face. One would have seen very little of his face, however; for when receiving audience, Pharaoh would wear a wig and a long artificial beard in imitation of the bearded gods of judgment. (Even the renowned female Pharaoh Hatshepsut, possibly the same woman who rescued Moses from the water, was said to have worn her beard when "in session.") A central and characteristic piece of the elaborate headdress was the diadem, the royal headband, to which was attached front and center the Uraeus, the golden image of the cobra rearing itself up just over the king's brow, symbolically poised to strike all those who opposed him. Incorporating the very presence of the two tutelary goddesses of Egypt, Wadjit (the cobra goddess of northern or Lower Egypt) and Nekhbet (the vulture goddess of southern or Upper Egypt), the diadem itself was regarded as being invested with inherent divine power. For the Egyptians, it was only fitting that the regalia and trappings of the court expressed the inestimable glory and power due the office. And if those seeking audience with Pharaoh felt intimidated by all this, it only meant that they were getting the point.

The time to speak to Pharaoh would come soon—but not too soon. First, on being prompted, Moses and Aaron would have been expected to lift their arms up in the air as they proceeded forward, much as any religious devotee might raise his arms in prayer or worship. Then, when they were close enough, they would have been expected either to bow deeply before the king or, more likely, fall prostrate to the ground and kiss the floor before Pharaoh's feet. Then, on rising, before even a word of business could be uttered, they would have had to recite a memorized hymn of praise to Pharaoh as a kind of preamble. One such standard hymn, which I offer in a highly abridged version, goes something like this:

> You are like Ra in everything that you do, everything happens according to the wish of your heart. We have seen many of your wondrous deeds, and we have neither seen nor heard anything equal to you. What way is there that you do not know? Who accomplishes all these things like you? When you commanded the waters to cover the mountains, the oceans immediately obeyed. In your limbs is Ra himself. You are the living image on earth of your father [the god] Atum. Your tongue

is enthroned in the temple of truth. God is seated on your lips. You are immortal and your thoughts shall be accomplished, and your words obeyed for ever and ever, O King and Master.

This was not a special way to merely flatter Pharaoh. Rather this is how *every* conversation with the Egyptian king was supposed to begin, including, presumably, the conversation initiated by Moses and Aaron. Of course, all the while we must remember that no one dared speak *to* Pharaoh. It was enough simply to speak in Pharaoh's presence. If and how he chose to engage his audience, well, that was entirely up to him.

The Man

But just who was this Pharaoh anyway? What do we know about him as a person, about his rule, his personality, and his exploits? The answers to these questions would undoubtedly shed much-needed light on our background knowledge to the Exodus. Unfortunately, we cannot credibly claim to know anything about this Pharaoh with certainty, simply because we cannot be certain about the identity of the Pharaoh of the Exodus in the first place.

But we can make a few good suggestions, based on an early and late dating of the Exodus, respectively. (Since space prevents me from going into a full-blown rehashing of the case for either an early Exodus or a late Exodus, I will assume both possibilities for the sake of argument.) On the assumption that the Exodus occurred in 1446 B.C., one might offer that Amenhotep II (1450–1425 B.C.?) was the ruler of the day (although he may not have acceded to the throne until a good twenty years after the Exodus, in which case the honor would go to Thutmose III).

According to an inscription from his stela of the Great Sphinx, Amenhotep "appeared as king as a fine young man after had become well developed, and had completed eighteen years in his strength and bravery." Indeed, his athletic prowess was legendary. As archaeologist Al Hoerth reminds us in his book, *Archaeology and the Old Testament*, Amenhotep ensured that his posterity remembered the athleticism of his youth. For example, it was recorded (but we must remember by whom!) that no one had arms strong enough to draw Amenhotep's bow. And when Amenhotep did fire his arrows, so it is said, he was able to penetrate three inches of copper—of course, he hit a bulls-eye every time. Then we have the accounts of how he, by himself, could row a boat faster than the same boat could be rowed by two hundred sailors of the Egyptian navy. Of course, if this bit is true, it is only because the captain of that boat had allowed the prince to win by, say, instructing one hundred of his two hundred men to row backward while the other one hundred rowed forward!

Needless to say, whatever personal issues may have beset Amenhotep II, low self-esteem was not among them. The first decade of his reign he spent waging campaigns against kingdoms to the north; the last decade of his reign (he died of unknown causes in his early forties) was relatively peaceful. From his surviving inscriptions, we learn little more except that he held nothing but contempt for non-Egyptians. A proud man and fiercely xenophobic, Amenhotep

II certainly provides a decent match with the Pharaoh described in the biblical account.

If, instead, we opt for a late-date Exodus of 1270 B.C., we are squarely within the reign of Rameses II (reigned 1279–1213 B.C.), also known as Rameses the Great. Of all Egyptian Pharaohs, none was greater or more powerful. His career was not only illustrious in terms of military exploits and building projects, but also exceptionally enduring—a whopping sixty-six years. If the Exodus took place under Rameses's watch, as the majority of late-date Exodus scholars imagine, then this interview occurred when the king was thirty-three years old, a mere seven years into his rule.

At the same time, these seem to have been a very active seven years. Within that window, Rameses had already subdued the marauding Sherden sea pirates and waged two highly successful campaigns against the Canaanites and Hittites to the north. The ruler himself was reported to have participated in battle, including a hand-to-hand bout with a Canaanite prince (again separating fact from self-aggrandizing fiction may not be so easy here). So if this was the Pharaoh of the Exodus, then Moses and Aaron were essentially confronting a young man who had already established himself as a remarkable military go-getter, exhibiting only unflinching resolution in taking on those who opposed him. In this case, we find more than a little irony here. If Yahweh had called Moses to bend this Pharaoh's ear in regard to the plight of the Israelites, we can hardly imagine a less pliable ear than a Type-A personality like Rameses.

The Message

Whoever the reigning Pharaoh might have been now facing Moses and Aaron, the two brothers have to pitch their idea of letting the Israelites go. Interestingly, Moses introduces his idea in a flatly declarative manner, citing the words of Yahweh as would a prophetic messenger: "Thus says the Lord (Yahweh), allow my people to go so that they might go and celebrate a festival to me in the wilderness" (Exodus 5:1). The preamble, "Thus says the Lord," is in fact a take-off on typical ancient Egyptian predications of divine speech. By opening his speech with this particular phrase, reminiscent of phrases like, "Thus says Horus" or "Thus says Osiris," Moses is not only introducing Pharaoh to the God of Israel for the first time but also putting the Egyptian ruler on notice that Israel's God is somehow akin to, and perhaps also in competition with, the gods of Egypt.

But make no mistake—the world of the gods has no such thing as friendly competition. When I was in eighth-grade English class, I remember learning that basically all stories could be classified according to one of only four types of conflict: man versus nature, man versus self, man versus man, and man versus society. If this is true, then the casual reader of the Exodus narrative could be forgiven for concluding that what is about to transpire is a conflict between one man (Moses) and another man (Pharaoh) over control of the Israelites. On a superficial level, that might be true—but only on a superficial level. It would also be missing the point. The real conflict—the real story behind the story of the Exodus—is not a conflict between Moses and Pharaoh, much less between the Israelites (the good guys) and the Egyptians (the bad guys). Instead, the real conflict is between Yahweh the Creator God and the pretentious deities of Egypt. To be sure, Moses and Pharaoh must play their respective roles within that conflict, namely, as priestly messengers representing their respective deities, but the bottom line has to do with issues of power and sovereignty in the realm of deity.

"Who is more powerful," the book of Exodus asks its readers, "the gods of Pharaoh/Egypt or the God of Moses/Israel?" Or, to put it in Pharaoh's own words: "Who is the Lord that I should pay attention to him and let Israel go?" (Exodus 5:2). True, we can almost hear the narrator's voice saying, "Don't worry, Pharaoh. You will receive an answer to your question soon enough!" But at this moment of history, Pharaoh considers the request itself an affront to everything he stands for, and responds accordingly.

The Response

Whatever Moses and Aaron were hoping to achieve that day, to say that the much-anticipated meeting did not go very well would be an understatement. Perhaps this is partially the fault of Moses himself, whose wording—the Hebrew makes clear—is both curt and demanding, more so than the wording that Yahweh himself had suggested! Not only does Pharaoh reject Moses and Aaron's bid, he also makes them pay for even daring to issue the insolent request. While earlier policy for the Israelites had provided straw for their brick-making task, now they have to both make the bricks *and* gather all their own raw materials, mud *and* straw (Exodus 5:4–14). In short, thanks to Moses and Aaron, the Israelites now have an increased workload but are forced to maintain an undiminished quota of bricks. Those who didn't meet quota, as countless ancient reliefs show us all too well, could expect to receive severe beatings. One can hardly imagine a more disastrous outcome from what initially seemed like a divinely initiated great idea.

As may be expected, when the Israelite supervisors catch wind of Pharaoh's new demands, they bring curses down on the heads of Moses and Aaron for their having exacerbated what was an already intolerable situation (Exodus 5:20–21). Feeling this intense pressure from their former supporters, Moses in turn takes his own complaint to Yahweh. Who can blame him? After all, Yahweh had put him up to all this in the first place.

In response, Yahweh makes clear to Moses that the apparent setback does nothing to decrease his resolve to deliver Israel. Nor does Yahweh imply that he intends to qualify his promise in light of presenting realities. Instead, the God of Israel simply repeats his commitment but now does so in more starkly theological terms.

God's Hand

First of all, Yahweh once again promises to accomplish the Exodus through a "mighty hand" (Exodus 6:1). A calculated choice of words, the phrase was clearly meant as a mocking response to pharaonic ideology that would constantly make much of Pharaoh's hand or forearm. (In biblical languages, the "hand" runs up to the elbow; so when Jesus shows Thomas the holes on his "hands," he is displaying not his palms, as Western art has typically portrayed the scene, but his forearms.) For example, in ancient depictions of the Egyptian king hovering over his cringing enemies, it is not uncommon to find the bullying Pharaoh represented with an out-stretched arm. Along the same lines, the Pharaohs were often keen to be known by their hands/arms. Pharaoh Hophra retained the title "Possessed of a Muscular Arm"; Rameses II himself, just discussed above, preferred to be known as "The Strong-Armed." Against this background, Yahweh's point is well taken. Inasmuch as Pharaoh's arm/hand symbolized his power and strength, Yahweh's expressed determination to deal with Pharaoh by his own hand is a way of saying that Israel's God intends to beat the king of Egypt at his own game—the game of power.

Likewise, Yahweh's promise to "stretch out his hand" (Exodus 7:5), as we will see in the next chapter, will become the basis for the image of Moses stretching out his hand over the waters of Egypt (Exodus 7:19). From that point on, the correlation between Yahweh's stretching out of his hand and Moses extending his hand recurs throughout the Exodus narrative (8:5–6, 16–17; 9:3, 15, 22–23, 29; 10:12–13, 21–22; 13:3, 9, 14, 16; 14:16, 21, 26–27, 31; 15:6, 9, 12; 17:9–16; etc.), so much so in fact that the difference between Yahweh's hand and Moses' hand becomes almost indistinguishable.

The logic of this correlation was not lost upon later biblical writers who continued to construe Moses' hand as a visible expression of Yahweh's saving power (cf. Deuteronomy 4:34; 5:15; 7:19; 26:8; Psalms 77:20; 136:11–12; Isaiah 23:11; Zephaniah 1:4). Even in the New Testament, when Matthew and Mark describe Jesus as "stretching out his hand" in response to the beseeching leper (Matthew 8:3; Mark 1:41), they are almost certainly portraying Jesus as a kind of Moses re-enacting a new Exodus through the act of healing the leper. (Much more can be said on all this, but it is covered in the companion volume to this book, *Finding Jesus in the Exodus*.) For now, registering this point is enough: Whenever we picture the well-known image of Moses stretching out his hands for Israel's redemption, the Scriptures would have us think of this as being almost an incarnation of God's own hand.

God's Name

A second point of interest has to do with Yahweh's claim that when he appeared to Abraham, Isaac, and Jacob, he revealed himself as El Shaddai, but not by his name Yahweh (Exodus 6:3). This is puzzling because it is patently untrue. To be sure, the God of the patriarchs did reveal himself as El Shaddai (traditionally rendered as God Almighty, Genesis 17:1; 35:11). Equally true is that he also revealed himself as Yahweh, even as far back as the time of the primordial couple, Adam and Eve (Genesis 4:1), with countless instances of the tetragrammaton (*YHWH*) throughout the Genesis narrative. What are we to make of this?

In my view, and in the view of a number of scholars, the crucial idea is bound up in a proper understanding of God's self-revelation. Technically speaking, the God of Israel did indeed reveal himself to the patriarchs as Yahweh. This was God's self-revealed name from the beginning, so that the giving of the name at the burning bush was not so much a new datum but rather confirmation of the divine identity for Moses' purposes. At the same time, the biblical narrative will go on to suggest that no one really *knows* this Yahweh personally apart from an experience of his saving acts—saving acts that will be revealed in short order through the plagues, Passover, and passage to come. In the most meaningful sense, therefore, the God of Israel promises that Moses and his people—and indeed the Egyptians themselves—will, on the far side of the Exodus, come to know the name of Yahweh in a whole new way.

Sometimes I will ask people I meet, "Do you know the Lord?" What I mean when I ask that question is not "Do you have factual knowledge about the Judaeo-Christian God?" but rather, "Do you *know* him? Do you know him experientially and in a saving way?" There is knowing and then there is *knowing*. I believe that Yahweh is drawing attention to precisely this distinction in Exodus 6:3.

This profound theological point not only deserves our reflection, but also, I think, challenges the way that many of us—perhaps even most readers of this book—think about God. For many people, because we are wittingly or unwittingly heirs of the Greek philosophical tradition, God is primarily an abstract concept. He is the one being who is all-powerful, all-knowing, all-good, and so forth. He is the God of all these abstract attributes. But here in Exodus 6, as in the usual biblical tradition, God does not self-reveal his essence (as if we could get our heads around the essence of God in the first place); instead, he only reveals himself in relation to what he intends to do for his people. God does not so much reveal himself in propositions (although there are some of these) but in his saving acts, and the saving act *par excellence* that will serve as a paradigm for all subsequent saving acts throughout redemptive history, which is about to occur under Moses' leadership.

This has important practical implications. God did not save us so that, once we get past all that saving bit (phew!), we could then enter into relationship where we could know him safe from within our ivory tower. Instead, God has saved us and continues to save us on a day-to-day basis so that we can know him precisely through the drama of salvation that is now unfolding around us. When we fail to appreciate the force of this point, we will inevitably divorce the entire business of knowing God from our everyday reality and reduce the living God to a sterile philosophical fact or a quaint theological datum. This is not to undermine the importance of doctrine, for doctrine is hugely important and painfully unappreciated in the contemporary Western church. But as important as doctrine is, we should also remember that doctrine does not save us. Doctrine provides the much-needed lenses for interpreting what God has done, is doing, and will do among, within, and on behalf of his worshipping community.

God's Covenant

The concept of "covenant" is another important piece of this interchange between Yahweh and Moses. The word itself is in fact used twice here: "I have also established my *covenant* with them, in order to give them the land of Canaan, the very land in which they lived as aliens. I have also heard the groaning of the Israelites whom the Egyptians are keeping as slaves and I have remembered my *covenant*" (Exodus 6:4–5).

The repetition is theologically significant. Although the suffering of the Israelites under Pharaoh's rod presumably would have been motivation enough for Yahweh to initiate the Exodus, divine compassion over Israel's wretched state was not the only precipitating cause of the Exodus. Nor, indeed, does this seem to have been the primary cause. Instead, the overriding motivation for Yahweh was his promise made to Abraham through a solemnly established covenant.

This requires its own explanation. Way back in Genesis 12 (as well as in Genesis 15 and 17), Yahweh initiated a covenant with Abraham which included a promise of land and seed (progeny). (By the term "covenant" I mean a solemn life-blood bond that binds two parties into a formal relationship of specified expectations.) According to the terms of the Abrahamic Covenant, God intended that the same seed that secured the land would also be a blessing for the nations. So when the descendants of Abraham, Isaac, and Jacob made their way down to Egypt in order to survive the years of famine in Canaan (thank you, Joseph), this move was to be finally understood not merely as a pragmatic strategy for survival but as God's appointed means for preserving the seed-line initiated under the Abrahamic Covenant. Having inaugurated the Abrahamic Covenant as a way of reversing the curse of the fall (Genesis 3—11), Yahweh was then— as the remainder of Genesis reveals—superintending the course of history behind the scenes to ensure the successful implementation of the covenant. In order to understand Genesis properly, we must see it not as the story of one debased human action after another (though on the surface it can read that way), but of God's advancing the goal of the Abrahamic promise despite and even through those debased human actions.

Now when we come to Exodus 1 with the story of the Israelites' oppression, we have every human reason to believe that the freight train of God's redemptive purposes has come to a grinding halt. As the story unfolds, however, we begin to see that this is only the appearance of things: God is moving forward after all, even through the suffering of his people. By linking the imminent Exodus with the Abrahamic Covenant, Yahweh's words in Exodus 6 frame this miraculous historical moment within a context that was larger than the immediate plight of the Israelites. Accordingly, Moses is being invited to rely on God's faithfulness not simply to the Israelites (as if God's people were an end unto themselves), but to the overarching missiological promise made to Abraham.

On this reading, we are to understand the Exodus not as an isolated event or an astonishing one-off event, but as a crucial step toward cashing out God's promise of salvation for the nations. Because this salvation in turn required a public revelation of divine power, Yahweh knows that the time has come to set the scene for this revelation by staging a tug-of-war over the Israelites—between the underdog Moses and the reigning and highly-favored champion, Pharaoh. Of course, as we shall see, this same underdog will have a trick or two—or ten!—up the sleeves of his extended arm. In the Exodus, the power of the false god Pharaoh becomes the foil for a demonstration of true power issuing from the true God Yahweh. Not just Israel but all the nations—including Egypt itself—are counting on Yahweh putting Pharaoh in his place.

The Snakes

With all this in mind, Moses and Aaron schedule a second appointment with Pharaoh (Exodus 7:8–13). This time the two brothers come not just with words but also with power, as is made clear when Aaron throws down his staff and it becomes a snake. At least it might have turned into a snake, but there are other options. For while the first instance of this miracle involved a *nāhāsh* ("snake"—Exodus 4:2–3), in this instance the Hebrew reads not *nāhāsh* but *tannîm* ("sea-monster," "dragon," "crocodile," but only secondarily "serpent"—Exodus 7:9–10). Some scholars have made a plausible argument that Aaron actually produces a crocodile to impress the great king. But I don't think we should overemphasize the semantic difference between *tannîm* and *nāhāsh*, since 7:15, with clear reference to the rod-turned-*tannîm* episode of 7:8–13, has Yahweh saying: "Go to the Pharaoh in the morning, just as he goes out to the water. Stand nearby at the bank of the river to meet him, and take in your hand the staff which had been turned into a snake (*nāhāsh*)." If the biblical writer used a different term, this is not to indicate a different kind of sign from the one demonstrated at Sinai but is an act of poetic license, giving the whole scene a more sinister cast.

What happens next has to be, in my view, one of the most surprising twists in the whole of Scripture. For just when one would think that Pharaoh would be wowed by Aaron's demonstration, Pharaoh's *hartōm* (magicians), the Hebrew equivalent of the Egyptian *hry-hbt* (priest lectors), step forward and—in a moment that is as disappointing as it is anti-climactic—duplicate the feat. Nevertheless, Aaron's snake proceeds to consume all the snakes of the competing

Egyptian magicians. So we imagine Moses and Aaron being at least partially gratified by the final outcome. Gratified perhaps, but far from satisfied, for Pharaoh remains unimpressed. The reason he remains unimpressed, Scripture goes on to tell us, is because his heart is hardened (Exodus 7:13).

The whole scene is as puzzling as it is odd. It also raises a handful of questions, not least the question as to how, if Aaron's staff is indeed transformed into a snake by divine intervention, can we explain the Egyptian magicians reproducing the same accomplishment. A handful of explanations have been proposed.

In the first instance, one might suppose that the entire story was fabricated along the lines of a far-fetched legend. Yet this is not immediately convincing. The problem here has to do with issues of genre and the text's expectations upon the readers (the same issue discussed in Chapter 3). Nothing about the scene marks it out from the rest of the narrative as a symbolic parable or otherwise fictitious product of a creative imagination. On the contrary, because the episode blends in so seamlessly with the larger section of the Ten Plagues, the only way to explain the former away as legend would be to apply the same scalpel of skepticism to the latter—a move that would, I think, serve only as a very last resort.

A second suggestion is that Pharaoh's magicians, precisely because they are magicians, are able to perform an illusion that gives the visual impression of their staffs turning into snakes. While this is possible, we would still be left to explain how Aaron's snake/staff manages to gobble up a series of illusions.

Another option, and in my mind more plausible, is that the magicians simply perform their trick by a demonic magic. Unless we rule out ahead of time the possibility of demonic interference in our everyday reality, I believe we should give this possibility serious consideration. Demonic phenomena are well-accepted aspects of daily life in modern-day Africa, and are, I think, becoming increasingly accepted in the Western world. (I recall recently listening to a radio interview on a secular AM station with a Chicago police officer who responded to a report of a family under demonic control. On his account, when he entered into the bedroom of the nine-year-old son, he found the poor boy quite literally walking backward up a wall—a phenomenon also witnessed by the family's heroic social worker and a hospital nurse.)

Another explanation relates to the fact that the cobras may have been manipulated. By applying pressure on the back of a cobra's neck, a skilled snake-handler can reduce the snake into a kind of hypnotic paralysis whereby it becomes stiff as a stick. When the snake-handler wishes to "bring them back to life," he simply rolls the snakes in his hands or drops them to the ground. Although the biblical narrative is completely uninterested in explaining how Pharaoh's magicians do what they do, I believe that this explanation is the most credible of all. In fact, it is quite possible that Aaron and Moses, knowing full well the abilities of a trained Egyptian snake-handler, may have anticipated this very outcome!

But neither Moses nor Aaron could have anticipated their snake consuming the snakes of Pharaoh's magicians. And here, I believe, is where we find the true point of the miracle. When I refer to the "point of the miracle," I should say right up front that I do not believe that this head-to-head competition between the Yahwehist and the Pharaohists was about who could do the coolest trick. I do believe it was about two competing storylines representing two competing and irreconcilable faith systems. For just as Jesus would later perform miracles as lived-out parables dramatizing God's saving intentions, the same kind of thing is occurring here. But in order to unpack the meaning of this miracle, we must first get our own handle on Aaron's staff and Pharaoh's cobras.

The Staff

In the ancient Near East, a person's staff was much more than simply a walking stick or a weapon (although it served both of these functions). Rather, when one acquired a staff, one expected to keep it for life, and it became part of one's life. Typically personalized with a chiseled insignia, a staff was an instrument used for authenticating personal identity, much as a driver's license or passport would be used today. In this sense, one's staff was an extension of one's personal identity. Likewise, Aaron's staff represented Aaron himself, even as Moses' staff represented his own person. More than that, because Aaron and Moses essentially functioned as priests in the service of Yahweh, their personal staffs also represented Yahweh.

As for the snake or cobra, we should realize that this much-feared reptile—precisely on account of its fierce power—was an object of worship in ancient Egyptian culture. This was all the more the case with the Uraeus resting on Pharaoh's forehead; as mentioned earlier, this metallic emblem was thought to embody not only Ra and Horus, but also Wadjet, the tutelary goddess of the northern half of the Egyptian kingdom. We might put it this way: If any physical object was greater than Pharaoh himself, it was the golden cobra on his royal headband, which was ultimately the very source of Pharaoh's glory, awesomeness, and strength. In the ancient context, when anyone thought of a cobra they also thought of Pharaoh—and vice versa.

The Meaning

Once we take stock of the symbolism of the various props in this scene, the meaning of the scene itself becomes patently clear. By approaching Pharaoh and then allowing their divinely invested staff to turn into a snake, Moses and Aaron were engaging Pharaoh and his magicians at their own game. True, when the magicians saw what the two elderly Hebrew brothers were able to do with their staff, they must have been at least mildly impressed. If you were there, you might have even seen them smile. But they would not have been overly impressed nor would their smiles last long, for they had already learned and practiced the very same art and with little effort were able to imitate the Hebrews' *tour de force*.

Yet when the first snake (the symbolic extension of Aaron and Moses' relationship and identification with Yahweh) went on to devour the other snakes (the symbolic extension of Pharaoh's connection and identification with the Egyptian gods), the effect must have been at least slightly disconcerting even for the most stubborn. Still, little did the Egyptians appreciate the force of this ominous omen. For just as Aaron's serpent "swallows" (*bāla'*) Pharaoh's serpents (Exodus 7:12), very quickly a time would come when Yahweh's earth would "swallow" (*bāla'*) Pharaoh's army in the waters (Exodus 15:12). Had Pharaoh been more open-minded to the possibility of Yahweh being greater than himself and his gods, perhaps his reaction would have been different. But Pharaoh was not quite prepared to go there yet.

Some people go through life saying to God, "Show me your ways, O Lord"; others go through life saying to God, "I'll show you!" Pharaoh belonged to the latter category. As a result, the battle between the God of Moses and Aaron on the one side and the gods of Pharaoh on the other was now fully engaged.

A final comparison with the Justina Pelletier case may help us to grasp the significance of this moment. When the director of the Christian Defense Coalition approached the governor of Massachusetts on the street and referred to Justina's inability to go to church so long as she was under the auspices of the state, he was of course appealing to the constitutional provision forbidding the state from impeding "the free exercise of religion." It was a shrewd argument, since in the United States the Constitution has the final say. But what kind of argument can Moses and Aaron make in their own bid to exercise their religion in a land with no Constitution or Bill of Rights, and where only one man has the final say? In short, they must appeal to a still higher power. "Either let the Israelites go to worship their God," they more or less say to Pharaoh, "or else you and your so-called gods will have to do business with him." Walking away from the royal snakefest, Pharaoh's response in so many words is this: "Fine. I'll take my chances!"

Taking their staff, Moses and Aaron go home. But as they make their way through the streets, they must be wondering what exactly Yahweh might do next. Pharaoh is clearly digging himself in. And if they have any hope of changing his mind, then Yahweh will have to do something big. As it turns out, something *big* is just around the corner.

PLAGUES

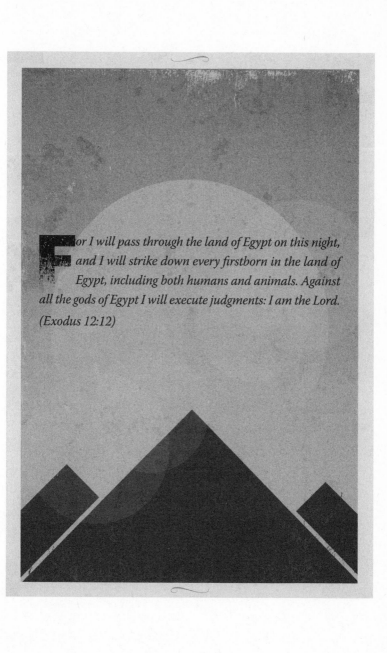

For I will pass through the land of Egypt on this night, and I will strike down every firstborn in the land of Egypt, including both humans and animals. Against all the gods of Egypt I will execute judgments: I am the Lord. (Exodus 12:12)

The other day as I was preparing to go on a trip overseas, I was moving a very full garbage can to the front curb for pickup. Dragging it to the street, I lifted the lid to add one last item only to discover the inside crawling with dozens (if not hundreds) of maggots. I don't know why I find those little white worms so revolting, but I do. Once back inside the house, I washed my hands in the biblical sense—up to my elbows!

The next step was to scare up a couple of long extension cords in case we would have a hard rain while I was gone. Where we live, thunderstorms often cause the streets to flood. Before we know it, the mulch chips we just laid down on the front garden beds could turn into little untethered canoes. The shoreline of the river—the torrent rushing along where the street used to be—makes its way inch by inch up the gently sloped front yard toward the house. At this point, the basement would be completely flooded were it not for our sump pump. Trouble is, at stormy times like these—for reasons I still do not completely understand—we also regularly lose power, which, apart from our generator, would mean no more working sump pump and no more dry basement. But just having a generator doesn't help if I don't have the extension cords to run the power from the generator outside to the sump pump in the basement. So whenever the rain picks up, my gut slowly begins to tighten while my mind automatically goes through a mental checklist (generator has gas? extension cord? functional sump pump?). Any weak link in the chain means a flooded basement. You might understand why I have a mild dread of storms.

In the middle of these preparations, my wife returned from the pharmacy where she had bought me medications that would preempt illnesses that Westerners sometimes endure when they go where I was going. While I was gone, I knew she probably would spend time with a friend of ours who years ago had contracted Lyme Disease—she and her whole family, indeed her whole subdivision. In this case, the neurological, physical, and emotional effects of the tick-borne illness were profound. I love being outdoors, but in certain parts in the United States I will not hike without a good hat and long pants tucked into my socks. Who could have predicted fifty years ago that one day getting into the "great outdoors" would be so risky?

For all its beauty and grandeur, our fallen created order can also be simultaneously revolting, fear-inspiring, and downright toxic. This is simply a fact of our everyday experience. But in the story of the Ten Plagues, a gripping story within the already gripping Exodus story, created phenomena are transformed into things grotesque and terrifying beyond all human experience. Nature spins out of control.

To be clear, however, the story of the plagues is not at all about nature. I say this because many stories have been written about the

great conflict between humanity and nature. This is an especially prevalent theme in much of American literature. (Consider, for
example, *Moby Dick*, a story of man versus whale.) Something is
awe-inspiring about dealing with an external reality bigger than ourselves. But the fictional story of *Moby Dick* and the biblical account
of the Exodus have a major difference. In the former, nature (more
exactly, "Nature") is essentially an autonomous force in its own right;
however, the Bible has no such abstract concept as "Nature." For the
Jews, nature was but a prop in Yahweh's outstretched hand. Thus,
while the plagues were issued to remind humanity of the "external
reality . . . bigger than ourselves," in this case that reality is Yahweh.

Modern Scholarship on the Plagues

Perhaps not surprisingly, a good number of Bible critics believe
that with this story of the Ten Plagues all we have is *story*—that is,
a fanciful construct of a creative imagination. For these readers, it
simply beggars belief that Moses should be able to affect catastroph-
ic changes in the ecosystem and in the atmosphere, not to mention
control the sunshine and spike Egypt's infant mortality rate. The
story defies scientific explanation—enough said. For them, this is
great fiction, perhaps, but not so convincing as historical reportage.
We might call this view the mythological approach.

Taking a different tack, others have been persuaded by an explanation that grants some level of historicity to the biblical narrative but attempts to square it with what we might expect from the
so-called laws of nature. Somewhat recently, for example, Barbara
Sivertsen has argued that eight of the first nine plagues can be ex-

plained by a late seventeenth century B.C. eruption in the Mediterranean Sea, which in turn produced a tsunami, which in turn wreaked havoc on the Egyptian ecological system. (She is no doubt influenced by Egyptologist Hans Goedicke, whom we will discuss in Chapter 7.) But an especially influential instance of this broader approach can be found in the 1957 study by the German scholar Greta Hort who argued that a good number of the plagues could be explained by natural processes. On her reconstruction, one year the Nile River was hard hit by excessive flooding, which caused kicked-up sediment and a good dose of alien bacteria from nearby lakes to fill the river. The sediment and bacteria in turn gave the river a red tint (accounting for the river's blood-red color as reported in the first plague), and also led to a water-oxygen imbalance that killed the fish. Once the water became polluted from dead fish, the frogs eventually had to move to dry land (second plague). These nevertheless perished on account of having been contaminated by anthrax from the fish, thereby attracting mosquitoes and stable flies (third and fourth plagues). Since these insects also happened to be carrying anthrax via the frogs, eventually the livestock also began dying (fifth plague), while the humans also suffered physical symptoms from the same (sixth plague). Unrelated to the first six devastations, the plagues of hail and locusts (seventh and eighth) were naturally occurring events. The ninth plague could be chalked up to desert sandstorms (*khamsin*), which have been known to last hours or even a few days. The death of the firstborn (tenth plague) could also be explained along natural lines. Let's call this very tidy explanation, variations of which go back way before the twentieth century, the naturalist or rationalist approach.

Such an approach has both strengths and weaknesses. As for strengths, Hort has at least explained how a series of successive steps within a hypothesized ecological disaster could make sense of Exodus's plot sequence. Historians tend to prefer explanations that can move us from A to B, from B to C, from C to D, and so on. In this respect, the scenario offered by Hort is an attractive option. Moreover, since this explanation does not make any special demands for believing the miraculous (so it has been argued), it should be preferred to a solution that ascribes miraculous elements.

Hort's reconstruction has significant weaknesses, however. In the first place, it provides only a partial explanation. That is, it can only speak to an interrelationship between the first six plagues. The next three plagues (hail, locusts, and darkness) must be regarded as random occurrences; and to attribute the tenth plague (death of the firstborn), as Hort does, to a high infant mortality rate, well, that just doesn't wash at all. Second, if we were to subscribe to this rationalist interpretation, we would be forced either to conclude that Aaron and Moses were self-deceived but nevertheless amazingly lucky in predicting the plagues—not to mention amazingly lucky in their timing (Exodus 7:17–19; 8:1–5, 16; 9:1–6, 13–21; 10:4–6; 11:4–8)— or discount their involvement altogether as a fictitious add-on. If we suppose the latter, we are ultimately contemplating only a variation of the mythological approach. If we retain the Hebrew brothers' involvement and imagine the former, we are being asked to give credence to a series of events so coincidental that—quite apart from whether we are dealing with divine intervention or simply an intense manifestation of naturally occurring phenomenon—we might as well use the term "miracle." Since the miraculous was exactly what the rationalist approach was hoping to avoid, the argument is ultimately self-defeating.

Ultimately, both the mythological approach (the plagues are purely fictive) and the rationalist approach (the plagues can be scientifically explained) make too many demands of the text. If the core of the Exodus is historical and the plagues are not historical, then we must ask what the point is of the biblical writer inserting, rather misleadingly, a mythological plague narrative within the context of a historical, Exodus narrative. Alternatively, if the plagues did have some basis in specific events in Egypt's natural history, then either we are merely talking about a difference in miraculous degree, or we are saying that completely normal events have been passed off as prophetically initiated miracles with *lots* of editorial freedom. Solving one set of intellectual problems sometimes creates another set that leaves us in no better position.

Against both of these approaches, I again suggest that we take the text at face value: The natural phenomena exhibited in each plague fell under the mediatorial control of Aaron and Moses. At this point I make no claims along the lines of "here is exactly what you would have seen had you been there." Nor will I even attempt to issue a scientific explanation. Frankly, I believe that as we consider the Ten Plagues (transcending our ordinary experience of garbage-bin maggots and Lyme Disease), we find ourselves in territory beyond the sphere of empirical science. Lots of things fall outside our explanatory paradigms, including, for example, clinically proven out-of-body and near-death experiences. Whereas the thoroughgoing naturalists among us must shrug their shoulders at this point, I am willing to believe that the Creator God himself was disrupting the delicate balance of created order.

The Meaning of the Plagues

But why would a good and loving God be interested in doing all these things anyway? In the last chapter, I attempted to shed light on the contest of cobras by appealing to relevant Egyptian backgrounds. There I argued that when you understand what a staff would mean to the average ancient Jew, as well as what the cobra would mean to the average ancient Egyptian, the pieces of the puzzle begin to fall into place. In this chapter, I will explain how an understanding of the plagues against both their Egyptian and Jewish backgrounds helps us to see how the Ten Plagues held two levels of meaning: one level applicable to God's people and another level applicable to the people of Egypt—both meanings would have been completely understood by the Jews.

The Ten Plagues were a series of symbolic actions, enacted parables if you will, directed against Pharaoh and the gods of Egypt. At least this was how second-Temple Judaism saw it. For example, in a first-century B.C. text called the *Wisdom of Solomon* (part of the biblical Apocrypha), the author clearly states that the plagues were intended as acts of judgment against the Egyptian idols. Likewise, in *Jubilees*, another Jewish text of roughly the same period, we find similar sentiments. True, one may argue that these views are only interpretations and should not be offered as evidence for the original meaning of the Ten Plagues. But we have to remember that traditions must start somewhere. And if these two texts from the Hellenistic period saw the plagues as judgments specifically issued against the Egyptian gods, then to infer that this point was widely granted in the day would not be a stretch. Again, this does not necessarily mean that it was exactly what the biblical writer had in mind, but consistent interpretive traditions must find their source somewhere. And why not from the beginning?

For what it's worth, the Bible itself indicates that the plagues should be understood precisely along these lines. One might think of Exodus 12:12, "For I will pass through the land of Egypt on this night, and I will strike down every firstborn in the land of Egypt, including both humans and animals. Against all the gods of Egypt I will execute judgments: I am the Lord." If the tenth plague was a judgment issued against "all the gods of Egypt," then this suggests that the previous nine plagues were likewise unleashed with the same intent (see also Numbers 33:4). Naturally, Yahweh engages in this one-upmanship not for the benefit of the gods, but rather for all the people who have learned to depend on them to their own peril. Confronting the gods of Egypt as masquerading impostors, the God of Israel intends through the plagues to remove the masks one at a time, leaving the same gods exposed to mocking ridicule. (Interestingly enough, in Exodus 10:2 the word "to mock" is synonymous with judgment.) Far from being interested in vindictively inflicting physical pain on the Egyptians, therefore, Yahweh is concerned to make a lasting impression that, on a symbolic level, both publicly humiliates the so-called gods and demonstrates Yahweh's sovereignty over them, especially in their supposed areas of responsibility.

These ten plagues also had a message for the Jews who knew the creation story, handed down from generation to generation through oral tradition. In fact, one of the interesting things about the plagues is the way in which they build on the biblical account of creation. Echoes of Genesis have already been resounding in the pages of Exodus in several places. For example, when we read about Moses' mother floating her infant son in a pitch-and-tar-covered *tēbāh* (chest) (Exodus 2:3), we are being invited to think of an earlier *tēbāh*, also cemented with pitch and tar: the ark of Noah (Genesis 6:14). Like Noah, Moses would also be saved through water. (In 1 Peter 3:18–22 the deliverance of Noah is explicitly identified as a type of Christian baptism "which also saves"; by extension, Moses' floating crib may also have been understood by early Christians as prefiguring baptism.) Since the Noah story in Genesis 6 is, in fact, a story of a reboot of a creational system that crashes pretty quickly after the fall of Genesis 3, we expect that the birth of Moses likewise presages new creation. Indeed, for just as the very first dry ground appeared out of the water as a platform for new life (Genesis 1:9–10), so too baby Moses would emerge out of the water later to become the basis for a new life for Israel. Following now a good number of scholars, I shall argue that the plagues are part of this re-creation story, albeit in a curious and somewhat paradoxical way.

So then, the Ten Plagues do double duty. For the astute Egyptian observer, they effectively demote the gods from their assigned positions of prominence. For the astute Jew, they finally put Yahweh in his proper place as King of the universe. If you are about to trust this God as redeemer, first you better nail down his identity as Creator.

First Plague: Water to Blood (Exodus 7:14–24)

The Nile River was many things to many people. It served as the Egyptians' central supply for drinking water as well as water for their crops. Teeming with life, the Nile also provided a staple food source for Egyptian peasants along the shore and a source of income for the local fishing industry. Finally, the river was an important component of Egypt's infrastructure; it was a water super-highway useful for transporting goods from north to south and back again. In many respects, the Nile was the spinal cord that held the kingdom of Egypt together; break the river and the kingdom itself would be paralyzed.

As I have already discussed in Chapter 2, the Nile's importance explains the prominence of Hapi, the female-breasted male god of the Nile and fertility, within the Egyptian pantheon of gods. We have already witnessed Moses' would-be adoptive mother going to the Nile to bathe (Exodus 2:5), an action that I suggested may have been part of a cultic gesture to Hapi, calculated to enhance her abilities to conceive. During the course of the plagues, Moses is instructed to meet Pharaoh as the latter makes his way to the water, which is also likely an act of devotion to the Nile god (Exodus 7:15; 8:20). Thus the text of Exodus provides ample evidence of Hapi worship at Egypt's highest levels. Given the Egyptian worldview, this makes complete sense. Because all of life revolved around Hapi and his river, for Pharaoh to remain within Hapi's good graces was crucial.

After Moses and Aaron turned the Nile to blood (Exodus 7:14–24), however, the river no longer clearly belonged to Hapi after all. By raising his staff (which, we recall, was more or less Yahweh's ID or business card) and striking the Nile's waters, Aaron was clearly acting in the name of a foreign god. As the water turned red and the fish started floating to the top, suffocating for lack of water, Hapi was suddenly appearing very hapless. Whether or not Pharaoh was willing to take Yahweh's point on board (he was not, according to Exodus 7:22–23), the Lord God's sovereignty over the Nile god was ("Take it or leave it, Pharaoh!") one of the main points of the first plague.

If with this first plague the God of Israel was thrusting a taunting index finger into Hapi's chest, he was also with the other hand pointing back to himself and the primordial story of creation. Consider the wording of Yahweh's command to Aaron through Moses: "Taking your staff, stretch out your hand over the waters of Egypt: over the streams and canals, and over the ponds and all the reservoirs (*miqewēh*) of water" (Exodus 7:19). The Hebrew term, translated here as "reservoir," also occurs in Genesis 1:10 in reference to the sea, from which the land is separated through the creative act. So then, just as the Creator God had formed the "reservoirs" to hold water in Genesis 1, now in Exodus 7 he was essentially removing the water, originally an integral part of the goodness of creation, and putting something ugly and putrid in its place. Likewise if God created the fish in order that they might increase and fill the waters (Genesis 1:21–22), now those same fish, once beautiful in their original living form, were washing up as carcasses on the blood-drenched shore.

The true Creator was hitting the reverse button on his own video, as it were.

Second Plague: Frogs (Exodus 8:1–15)

Recognizable by a female human body with a frog's head, Hekhet, the goddess of the frogs, was also a fertility god. Whether or not this particular function is immediately relevant to the plague of frogs is unclear. More likely, the God of Israel seems to have been taunting Hekhet along a different set of lines. By multiplying the frogs, Yahweh draws attention to the goddess as one who patently fails to maintain the appropriate population level of frogs along the river, as was her prescribed duty. As a result, anyone used to believing that Hekhet was in control of the frogs (and anything else for that matter) would be forced to reconsider their position.

The plague of frogs may include a polemic on another level as well. Because Hekhet was the consort of the Egyptian creator god Khnum, a slap on Hekhet's wrist may have also been, by extension, a poke at Khnum. The Egyptians and the Israelites had two very different accounts of creation. Now that the frogs had proliferated in a conspicuous way, an Egyptian creator god and his girlfriend have suddenly been compromised.

Of course, frogs were also part of Yahweh's good creation. I am not certain whether these amphibians would have fallen under the ancient Jewish category of water creatures (Genesis 1:20) or land animals (Genesis 1:24). (Modern biology will have its own answer on this one, but our categories are the same ones the ancients used.) In any event, by getting into people's kneading-troughs and beds, the

proliferating frogs were transgressing the normal creational boundaries set for them (Exodus 8:3–4). Once upon a time, somebody's
fastidious grandmother came up with a useful saying: "A place for
everything, and everything in its place." This is actually not too far
from a basic principle of creation that holds that the transition from
chaos to order is marked by the imposition of boundaries. That the
frogs were invading the domain of humans, who were ordinarily
supposed to have the task of ruling the creatures (Genesis 1:28), was
evidence enough that that part of creation had now gone badly awry.

Third and Fourth Plagues: Gnats and Flies
(Exodus 8:16–32)

After an inundation of frogs, a plague of gnats might seem un-
derstated. Yet the traditional translation of the Hebrew *kinnim* as
"gnats" is not entirely certain. The term may in fact refer to a wide
variety of other, more aggressive insects, including vermin, maggots, or lice. The last of these was an especially irksome problem
in ancient Egypt. (In case you're wondering, the reason why many
Egyptians kept clean-shaven heads and faces had to do with their
concern to avoid lice infestation.) As for the polemical point of
this particular plague, I confess that I am unsure. This is hardly a
deal-breaker for my argument, for we only know so much about
how Egyptians looked at these things.

The fourth plague involved descending swarms of horseflies
(although the Hebrew does not rule out the possibility that these
were actually mosquitoes). The insects would have been a painful
nuisance to both man and beast. We can only imagine the profound

sense of helplessness settling in on the Egyptians as they were overcome by thick clouds of these insects. Of course, bug spray had not been invented yet, and any kind of homemade fly-swatter would certainly have proved to be ridiculously futile.

Some have suggested that the plague of flies was Yahweh's answer to the Egyptian god Kheprer, symbolized by a flying beetle. In the earliest extant Egyptian creational account in the Pyramid Texts (the late third millennium B.C.), Kheprer is identified as the creator god. (You may now be confused at this point on the identity of the Egyptian creator god, but the Egyptians had various and conflicting accounts of creation.) In the relevant account of creation, a mound begins to emerge out of the chaotic waters, and on that mound Kheprer comes into existence—much like Dr. Who—through an act of self-generation. This narrative tidbit explains the god's name, for the Egyptian root *hpr* means "come into existence." There is a clear comparison between the Egyptian and Hebrew creational accounts (in both narratives, land emerges out of the deep like a surfacing submarine) and the respective names of the creator god and Creator God ("He Who Comes into Existence" and "I Will Be What I Will Be"). However many desperate prayers were muttered to Kheprer during this plague, "He Who Comes into Existence" was impotent to stay the overwhelming power of Yahweh. Meanwhile, the proper proportion and order of creation had once again been violated. The advent of insect swarms, well beyond ordinary experience, indicated divine displeasure and a fracturing of the cosmos's delicate balance.

Fifth Plague: Livestock (Exodus 9:1–7)

The plague against the livestock functions on several levels. First, we must remember that in an agrarian society like ancient Egypt, livestock accounted for a major portion of a rural householder's personal assets. To touch the Egyptians' livestock was to touch their wallets. In addition to being a precious commodity, livestock were also useful for providing milk and meat, as well as for use in projects requiring heavy lifting, dragging, or carrying. The impact on daily Egyptian life of losing the livestock would have been immense.

The most imposing member of this animal set is the bull which, by virtue of its sheer physical power, was regarded in Egypt as an object of worship. Apis worship revolved around sacred bulls. The major deities of Ptah and the solar god Re were also regularly represented as bulls. Moreover, certain goddesses took on bull-like characteristics, including Isis (who wore a pair of cow horns) and Hathor (whose whole head had a bovine form). To the northeast, in the Levant, a similar fascination with bulls was coordinated with the worship of the biblical fertility god Baal. (Vestiges of the same bull/fertility worship can still be found in Israel today on ancient stone engravings depicting crescent-shaped horns, a form that also inspired a familiar symbol of Islam, the crescent.) By inflicting a deadly disease on the bovine, among other livestock, Yahweh was sending a clear signal that all these gods were, well, a bunch of bull.

According to Scripture, on the sixth day of creation God created (1) livestock, (2) creatures that move along the ground, and (3) wild animals (Genesis 1:24). Sharing the same day of creation as humanity itself, such animals belonged to a special category. In other words, these animals and humans share a certain kinship, as can be attested to by anyone who has had to put down their horse or dog. Now by taking out the Egyptians' livestock, the Creator God was essentially un-creating what he had created. What was the point so far as the Jews are concerned? Simply this: "The Lord maketh and the Lord taketh away."

Sixth Plague: Boils (Exodus 9:8–12)

With the sixth plague, divine judgment circles in from external realities into personal space. While the first four plagues affected the Egyptians' resources and environment, and the fifth plague struck their living property, this is the first plague to impact the human body directly. To imagine this plague, we only need envision a broad-sweeping pandemic of painful shingles or chicken pox, conditions that are incurable, debilitating, and publicly manifest. The intensifying judgment of Yahweh began to hit home on a new level.

A good number of scholars are convinced that this plague was also a symbolic swipe against the Egyptian deities. Although opinions differ as to which god or gods are implicated, one could do worse than propose the lion-headed Sekhmet. This god was in charge of inflicting epidemics as well as, paradoxically, curing them. Accordingly, Egyptian physicians honored Sekhmet as the god of their own guild. Many prayers must have been raised up to Sekhmet in those days. And, certainly, those prayers went unanswered.

On the sixth day, God created humanity in his own image (Genesis 1:26–27). While theologians over the centuries have debated as to exactly how humanity has been created in the *imago dei*, I suspect that ancient Judaism understood the concept of the image of God to include our physical bodies. (For the Jews, the High Priest was in a very real sense of the true image of God, and he was obviously a physical being.) In this case, a strike against the Egyptians' bodies now meant that God was partially taking back what he started in day six of creation: the formation of the perfect human body.

Seventh Plague: Hail (Exodus 9:13–35)

Anyone who has ever filed an insurance claim for hail damage to their otherwise impervious cars can testify to how destructive hail can be. And not just for cars—things like crops, infrastructure, and animals also can get extremely damaged in the wake of a bad hail storm. In the summer of 2013, in one fifteen-minute hail storm, a region of Germany experienced 3.8 billion U.S. dollars of hail damage. Modern-day Germany is, of course, an industrialized society. But in ancient Egypt where the economy was so heavily dependent on agriculture, hail was especially bad news.

For the Egyptians, this would have been bad news with a focused punch line. In Egyptian mythology, the term Ennead, going back as early as the Fifth and Sixth Dynasties (2500–2200 B.C.) refers to nine major interrelated gods occupying four generations: Atum, Shu, Tefnut, Geb, Nut, Osiris, Isis, Set, and Nephthys. Three of these are associated with weather: Shu, the god of the air; Tefnut, the goddess of moisture; and Nut, their daughter, the goddess of the sky. While there is no tight one-to-one correlation between the plague of hail and any of these three gods, this does not necessarily blunt the overall point—namely, that an entire third of Egypt's hallowed

Ennead proved useless in deflecting the blows of Israel's God. If hail was thought to fall under the jurisdiction of any one of these three gods, or some combination thereof, the authority of these same gods was now demonstrably empty.

Exactly how this plague deconstructs creation is an open point of discussion. Perhaps the Jews would have recognized this as a violation of the boundaries separating the waters above (Genesis 1:6–8; compare Job 38:22). Perhaps the creational rewind implicit in the destruction of the vegetation is more in view. In either case, where we end up is the same: de-creation.

Eighth Plague: Locusts (Exodus 10:1–20)

If the sight of hail was like a bad dream, locust (today's grasshopper) swarms were an absolute nightmare. As the Old Testament prophet Joel testifies (see especially Joel 1:1—2:11), in antiquity no occurrence was more frightening than a locust attack. Just as it can be today, the devastation caused by locust swarms in those days was quite extensive, potentially wiping out an entire year's worth of crops. In a world where the overwhelming majority of the population eked a subsistence level of existence and did not have the luxury of stockpiling food, a locust swarm could spell starvation and economic disaster.

Typically resorting to their mythology in order to cope with such troubling uncertainties as plagues, the Egyptians acquired a sense of control by turning to Senehem, the locust-headed god of the locusts and the supposed sovereign over locust attacks. Though a minor god in Moses' day, Senehem would in the much later Roman period morph into the more prominent Serapis. Perhaps Jews and Christians of that era interpreted the eighth plague as an anticipatory judgment against one of the few Egyptian gods who would go on to penetrate the broader Roman Empire. Yet coming back to Moses' day, that a minor god like Senehem should be targeted along with a fairly exclusive set of deities is curious. With this in mind, we grant that Yahweh may not have been singling out Senehem alone in this particular plague. After all, the extant Egyptian corpus indicates that all the gods shared responsibility for preserving Egypt's crops.

Locusts are also among the winged-creatures of creation (Genesis 1:20–23). Like the other creatures, they were meant to be ruled by humanity. Now in the eighth plague, they are the ones ruling. The world is turned upside-down. Sin has that effect.

Ninth Plague: Darkness (Exodus 10:21–29)

According to the text, Moses stretched out his arms and total darkness covered the land (save for the neighborhoods of the Israelites) for three days (Exodus 10:21–23). Although the absence of sunlight would not have posed any immediate physical threat to either the Egyptians or their material possessions, a "darkness that could be felt" must have had profoundly chilling effects (Exodus 10:21). It might seem that a few days of darkness would come as a welcome reprieve after having been afflicted by frogs, gnats, and painful boils. I am not so certain. For my part, I suspect I would prefer animal infestations and bodily discomfort to a psychologically terrifying reality in which the sun has gone missing until further notice.

As the plagues draw to a close, they are now zeroing in on the heart of the Egyptian religious system. At the core of it all was the solar deity, Ra. With the dawn of each new day, the rising sun would remind the Egyptians of Ra's preeminence among the gods. Just as the sun gives new life to each day, so too did Ra give life to the created order itself. As pointed out earlier, Ra found his chief embodiment in Pharaoh himself.

Confounding the god of the sun, the plague of darkness is not the first allusion to this kingpin among Egyptian gods. Earlier in the text, the biblical writer appears to be playing on the verbal similarities between the name Ra and the Hebrew word for evil, trouble, or wickedness: *ra'*. So, for example, following the dire results of Moses' first petition to Pharaoh, we read: "The Israelite foremen sensed that they were in trouble (*ra'*) when they were told, 'You must not reduce the quota of bricks required of you each day'" (Exodus 5:19). Some scholars see a double meaning here. To be in *ra'* was not only to be in trouble but also to be in thrall to the person of Ra and his oppressive ways. But now, through the plague of darkness, both Ra and his authority were being called into question.

A further symbolism is bound up in this plague. By causing the Egyptians to dwell in utter darkness, Yahweh was in effect turning over a spiritually blind Pharaoh, the representative head of a spiritually blind people, to the full effects of his sin. In this connection, I should mention that the sun and the moon were regarded as the two eyes of the great god Horus, the right and left eye, respectively. By covering over the sun and the moon, Yahweh had in a symbolic sense darkened both of Horus's eyes! In the prophetic literature, we learn that those who worship blind idols will eventually themselves become blind. Perhaps a similar parallelism between a blinded god and a blinded people also occurs here in the ninth plague.

Meanwhile, turning to the Genesis account, we immediately recognize a connection with the very first fiat of creation: "Let there be light" (Genesis 1:3). Whereas Yahweh's creational plan included separating this light from the darkness, making day and night, his rolling back of light in the ninth plague served to collapse the day into the night. This can only be understood as a reversal of the very act of the Creator God.

I think yet another layer is here, one that includes yet transcends Egyptian and Hebrew symbolic systems. Because darkness and death are almost universally associated with each other, the plague of darkness must also be seen as anticipating the tenth plague, the death of the firstborn. The same correspondence between darkness and death of the firstborn emerges in the synoptic gospels' account where the firstborn Son of God expires only after a deep darkness has descended on the land (Matthew 27:45; Mark 15:33; Luke 23:44–45). The evangelists, who were steeped in the Jewish scriptures and imagery, saw a natural analogy between darkness and final judgment, both for plague-enduring Egypt and for the Son of God who bore the "plague" on behalf of God's people. In early Christianity, the ninth plague looked forward to the Cross moments before Jesus' expiration, even as the tenth plague anticipated his death.

Tenth Plague: Deaths of the Firstborn
(Exodus 11:1—12:33)

The final and climactic supernatural event, the plague against the firstborn of Egypt, is not only the most devastating of all plagues but is also the most far-reaching in theological import. In order to understand why, I need to explain the nature of royal lineage in ancient Egypt. As in many ancient societies, Egypt perpetuated itself through primogeniture, that is, the practice of assigning a father's full inheritance to the firstborn son. Accordingly, since the pharaonic line was passed down from one generation's firstborn to the next generation's firstborn, any interruption of that lineage was deemed a threat to the throne itself. In addition to being a tragedy on a personal level, the death of Egypt's heir apparent would not only create conditions for political instability but would also raise questions regarding the current ruler's future trajectory and legacy.

This has not only political but also religious implications. We recall that Pharaoh was regarded as divine by virtue of his office, even as the king's firstborn son would have also been seen as a kind of god in the making. Indeed, as the human repository for all of Egypt's future hopes and dreams, the firstborn son was in some sense even more important than Pharaoh himself. If the only thing more important than any society's present is its future, then the death of Pharaoh's son, together with the death of countless firstborns among Egyptian men and animals, would have marked a significant turning point in the contest—a contest by now very much in the public eye—between Yahwehism and the religion of pharaonic Egypt.

More than that, the death of Pharaoh's son would have signaled clear and decisive defeat for the once-revered pagan pantheon. One of my favorite football announcers has a trademark phrase reserved for that one play in the game that essentially ensures victory for the home team: "And . . . there . . . is . . . your . . . dagger!!" In the Super Bowl match-up between Yahweh and the gods of Egypt, the death of Pharaoh's son was the "dagger" that even the most stubborn of Pharaohs could not deny. The game was up, the clock had run down, and the time had come to concede that Yahweh was superior to all gods.

From the Jewish perspective, the un-creation of the heir to the pharaonic throne, a royal and priestly office, would have been a kind of photographic negative of the creation of Adam, who, as the garden's ruler and mediator, also had royal and priestly prerogatives. In the final plague, life was withdrawn from the son of Pharaoh, widely touted as a son of god, just as in the final act of creation, life was given to Adam, the true Son of God. In symbolically identifying Pharaoh's stubborn allegiance to the Egyptian gods as an ongoing reversal of creation, Yahweh could have hardly offered a more theologically eloquent closing statement.

Putting It All Together

We cannot deny that on some level the Ten Plagues were a judgment directed against Pharaoh as representative head of the Egyptian people. But the plagues were no vindictive payback. Instead they produced, on the one hand, an unforgettably hard-hitting exposé of the gods, and on the other hand, a clear demonstration of

Yahweh's status as the true Creator God. The plagues were, in other words, a kind of revelation, symbolically reflecting on the nature of God and sin. As such, despite their sometimes horrific effects, the Ten Plagues were as much vehicles of mercy as they were vehicles of judgment. As a warning of even more serious eschatological judgment, they were calculated to jar the Egyptians into repentance. As manifestations of Yahweh's power, they were also designed to galvanize the Israelites' faith prior to the long journey ahead.

The practical theological implications of all this are hard to miss. First, the story of the Ten Plagues reminds us of idolatry's powerful grip. God had indeed hardened Pharaoh's heart (a curious concept that will be unpacked in the next chapter). Still, Pharaoh's stubbornness is not unique but rather a sharply lined sketch of fallen humanity's tenacious commitment to resisting God. The principle is simple. We humans will often go to extraordinary lengths before coming to terms with spiritual reality; the degree to which we can deceive ourselves is frightening. In short time or long, those who trust in idols will find out the truth eventually.

Second, the Ten Plagues give us some important insights into the nature of sin. Humans are the very climax of God's creation. Yet when we engage in sin (in thought, word, or deed), we are taking what is good and true and beautiful and turning it into something that is evil and false and ugly. Sometimes Christians think, "Well, if all I need to do is ask forgiveness, then maybe it's not so bad for me to . . ." and we fill in the blank. This inward reasoning can only get traction through an inadequate understanding of ourselves as created beings. As a whole and in all its parts, creation has a trajectory.

As created beings, we realize our destiny within this trajectory as we obey the one, true God. But when we give ourselves over to our idols, we reverse the creational path and in the process become, in a sense, a little less human. When you drive down the highway at high speed and then suddenly throw the transmission into reverse; you will seriously damage the car. So it is with us as created beings.

A final point: The Ten Plagues affirm that Israel's God was the true God and the Lord of all creation. The very Kingdom that Yahweh asserted in the royal fiats of "Let there be light," along with the other fiats that follow in Genesis 1, was the true and lasting Kingdom. That Kingdom was creation itself as it was ruled by Yahweh. Those who sought to oppose Yahweh as he advanced his Kingdom purposes would themselves be opposed and decisively vanquished. As becomes clear in the tenth plague, this rule applied even to the most powerful ruler in the world. No ruler or principality, human or demonic, had the wherewithal to obstruct the purposes of God. In the end, despite any appearance to the contrary, God would achieve the destiny of his Kingdom and his Kingdom people. In a world that often does not go our way, it is good to know that God is ultimately in complete control of everything from flooding to Lyme Disease. He is even the Lord and sustainer of all maggots—better him than me.

For those who had eyes to see and ears to hear, the Ten Plagues were revelatory stepping stones designed to lead Israel to spiritual maturity. Through each successive plague, Israel learned something new about the power of their saving God. Soon enough, the twelve tribes would find themselves in a passage to a trying physical journey, but the spiritual journey had already begun while they were still in Egypt. To attempt the one without the foundation of the other would have been disastrous. Yet the tenth plague and the proscribed Passover meal that accompanied it tied these two journeys together. With this final plague and epoch-marking meal, the long-awaited Exodus finally got underway.

PASSOVER

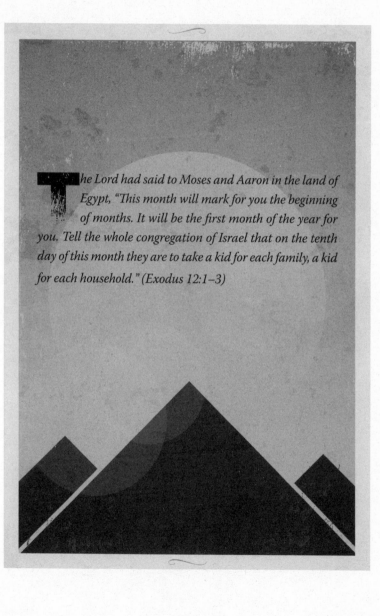

The Lord had said to Moses and Aaron in the land of Egypt, "This month will mark for you the beginning of months. It will be the first month of the year for you. Tell the whole congregation of Israel that on the tenth day of this month they are to take a kid for each family, a kid for each household." (Exodus 12:1–3)

A nother family road trip, another search for a place to eat. This time the issue wasn't BBQ versus KFC; this time the issue was whether we would find a place to eat at all. I admit we hadn't planned this one very well. Intending to be gone for nearly a week, we had just finished packing up the car with luggage and gift-wrapped presents for extended family members. The original plan was to leave bright and early in the morning, but one thing had led to another and now it was about 1 PM. When it comes to our family vacations, leaving half a day late is about par for the course.

Finally we were pulling out of the driveway. But no sooner were we on the road than I was reminded that no one had eaten lunch. Could we wait? No, apparently some of us were "starvarian." Having locked the front door for the third "final time," neither my wife nor I had the heart to turn back. Besides, we weren't sure whether we had anything to eat at home anyway. Even before we really got started, we were forced to stop for lunch.

This would not normally be a big deal except that we were traveling on Christmas Day. "Surely, at least a few places must be open on Christmas," we thought. And, surely, we were wrong. Cruising through the seemingly lifeless streets of Chicagoland, we were met with confirmation after confirmation that all the local restaurants and all the chains were closed. Of all holidays in America, Christmas is the most sacred. I guess I never really closely investigated it for myself, but this is true: Everything comes to a stop for this holiday.

Christmas is also a day when many people get very particular about what they eat. This is because Christmas dinner is one of those events when even the non-traditionalists among us suddenly become very traditional. Who's invited? When to eat? Where to eat? What to eat? Why did we go to all this trouble anyway? For many of us, most of these questions are implicitly answered ahead of time by family precedent. Consciously or unconsciously, we default to tradition in planning the main meal of December 25 because we intuit that this piece cannot be separated from the larger symbolism of the day. Specific expectations of food and festivities go hand in hand.

Of course, the same principle of festive food fixtures applies to Thanksgiving Day (*Turkey* Day), and to a lesser extent for other holidays like Easter (roast lamb) and the Fourth of July (cookout foods like hamburgers and hot dogs). New Year's Day is its own category, which depends on regional or ethnic backgrounds (e.g., black-eyed peas and collard greens for Southerners, corned beef and cabbage for the Irish). For each of these holidays, the standard meal became standard for a reason. In other words, each of these holiday menus has a story behind it, even if—in the case of Thanksgiving Day, for example—that menu has evolved over the years. In each case, we are accustomed to marking off special days with certain characteristic meals.

This is the very reason that my family and I were so flummoxed about our lack of eating options. It was Christmas Day, and we were slowing realizing that unless our prospects improved, we would be eating our "traditional Christmas Day dinner" out of some rest area vending machine just off the interstate. It just didn't seem right. There had to be another way.

Fortunately, we were able to find a Chinese restaurant open for business. I love Chinese food, but for this White Anglo-Saxon Protestant, a Chinese meal on December 25 was a clear break from the traditional turkey or ham dinner. On that day, we all had to be flexible given our circumstances; but as an unapologetic carnivore, I also knew that on Christmas Day I wasn't about to order a seafood or a vegetable-only dish. Flexibility has its limits. I urged everyone to order quickly and eat quickly so that we could get back on the road as soon as possible. I also reminded them to make sure not to over-order: We weren't in a position to add to an already packed van a bunch of white-cardboard containers filled with steaming leftovers. Have I mentioned that we didn't plan this one well?

A Family Road Trip Meal

As strange as it might sound, the ancient Jewish *pesah* (Passover meal) was something like this experience, in several respects. First of all, at the most obvious and superficial level, it was instituted the night of the Exodus as a kind of family road trip meal. Every household within Israel was to eat his sacred meal—no exceptions (Exodus 12:24, 47). Furthermore, God instructed these families that they must eat the Passover in haste with their staff in hand, sandals on their feet, and their "loins girded up" (Exodus 12:11). (Girding up the loins simply meant tucking the lower portion of one's garments into your sash so that your legs were free to move about easily and quickly, whether for the purposes of a journey or a battle.) The sense of urgency was so great, in fact, that they didn't even have enough time to make the bread properly, that is, by giving the loaf time to rise through the slow-working yeast. This time the ancient analogue to microwavable bread was to be the rule. So the Jewish Passover was not quite a carry-out meal, but almost. The Israelites needed to be ready to go at a moment's notice.

Second, like our Chinese Christmas meal, the *pesah* was characterized by both fixed traditions and flexibility. For example, in the first installment of the Passover, the Israelites were to eat a *seh*, a lamb or kid goat from the herds. Later on, however, provisions were made for eating a calf (Deuteronomy 16:2). Similarly, whereas boiling the meat is strictly forbidden in Exodus 12:9, Deuteronomy 16:7, legislation reflecting a later time, allows that the meat be boiled (so the Greek translation's understanding of *bšl*). Other variations, introduced as concessions to the Israelites' changing cultural realities, caused the *pesah* to evolve over time.

This should disabuse us of the notion that the *pesah* was a rigidly timeless ritual. The first Passover meal would have been very different from the Passover meal of the prophet Zechariah in the sixth century B.C., which in turn would have been very different from the Passover celebrated by Jesus in the first century A.D. In fact, we're not even sure about the details of Jesus' famed Passover. The best we can do is reconstruct it with evidence from the later (in some cases, much later) rabbinic traditions. Yet all the same, throughout the centuries, Passover had a common core: given the pedagogical nature of the meal, one might even say a common core curriculum. Some things changed; other things remained unmovable fixtures of the feast.

Third, the Passover meal entailed—to a degree far exceeding our modern holiday dinners—a deep symbolism that defined the holiday as a whole. As we unpack that symbolism in this chapter, we will soon understand why ancient Judaism considered Passover to be so important. If, in our day, the Fourth of July celebrates the birth of a nation, and if New Year's Day marks the fresh start of a new calendar year, and if Thanksgiving and Christmas both commemorate a story from the past (though very different stories!), and if Easter looks forward to the great eschatological event of the future; then ancient Judaism's *pesah* signified all these things rolled into one. The commemoration of Israel's birth, the inauguration of a new calendar year, reflection on redemption past, anticipation of redemption future—all of this was bound up in *pesah*. For centuries, down to the time of Jesus and beyond, Passover was not simply a festival: It was *the* festival.

A Profoundly Important Event

"All well and good," you might be saying to yourself, "but what does all this have to do with the Exodus?" In a word: everything. The Passover meal is important not because it tells us what the Israelites happened to eat during their last night in Egypt. Instead, it was a carefully designed ritual pre-enactment of what was about to happen very soon after the first Passover meal. Understand the Passover and you will understand the theological whys and wherefores of the Exodus. Miss this piece and you are left with little more than a story about how the good guys got away from the bad guys with no particularly clear idea as to the "so what?" For the Jews, the Exodus was not only a historic event; it was also a message. Get a handle on the who, when, where, what, and why of the meal, and you've almost reached the bottom line of one of the greatest redemptive events in history.

Some of this already becomes clear when we consider the position of the Passover story, including the tenth plague and accompanying meal (Exodus 11:1—13:16), within the larger narrative. On even a brisk reading of the text, we notice that this section is straddled on the one side by the account of the first nine plagues and on the other side by the report of the Exodus itself. So situated, the Passover story is like a bridge connecting the long, drawn-out confrontation with Pharaoh to the Exodus itself. In retrospect, we see the tenth plague, the only plague finally to persuade Pharaoh, succeeding where the first nine plagues came up short. In retrospect, too, the first nine plagues almost seem to have been merely Yahweh's clearing of the throat for that which would be symbolically announced through the decisive tenth plague. This final plague, commemorated in the Passover, would finally secure Israel's release. More than that, as we shall see, the tenth plague turns out to be not only the crowbar that freed Israel from Pharaoh's grip but also the steel reinforcing rods that undergirded the foundation of Israel's entire religious system.

Before exploring these issues, we need to consider two dangling concerns that have troubled readers of the Exodus down through the centuries. Both have to do with Yahweh strangely intervening in the lives of Pharaoh and the Egyptians. While I make no claim to resolve all the difficulties of the Exodus in this book, there are two loose ends that I would prefer to tie up as best I can: the so-called plundering of the Egyptians and the hardening of Pharaoh's heart.

Christmas Come Early

On the night of the Exodus, when the Israelites were instructed to request valuable objects from their Egyptian neighbors (Exodus 11:2–3), they not only complied with the request but were also handsomely rewarded for doing so. This raises two questions. First, why did Yahweh require the Israelites to ask for a handout? (Wasn't God powerful enough to provide for the Israelites apart from the Egyptians?) Second, more perplexingly, why did the Egyptians respond so favorably? (Financial solicitation is hard enough when it comes to asking people sympathetic to the askers or their cause, so how are we to explain such across-the-board generosity from those who are patent outsiders?) These are good questions.

And, I think, we have some good answers. First, we need to be clear as to what exactly the Israelites were asking for. While many readers have supposed, no doubt misled in part by several major translations, that the Israelites were requesting little more than some jewelry pieces, this is not what the Hebrew noun in question means. The term *kēli* in Exodus 11:2 typically denotes "vessels" or "utensils" or "tools," and we have no reason to interpret it any differently here. Elsewhere, we learn that the Israelites also inquired after articles of clothing (Exodus 3:22; 12:35). If every Israelite family was diligent in complying with this memo, the total collection would have been considerable. When our family prepares for Christmas on the road, we have to pack the van carefully to make room for all those brightly wrapped boxes. The same must have been true for the Israelites as they loaded up the donkeys and oxen!

Given that this plundering is referred to three times in the narrative (Exodus 3:21–22; 11:2; 12:35), with the first instance occurring in Moses' call, we cannot treat this transaction as last-minute afterthought. No, we find a high level of divine intentionality here. But if so, what then was the intention? I would like to suggest a three-fold rationale.

First, the biblical text clearly uses language that frames the transaction between resident Egyptians and departing Israelites as a plundering, even a mugging. From this we infer that Yahweh is affecting retributive justice. The Egyptians had been exploiting the Israelites for centuries by forcing them into unpaid labor, and the time had come for Israel to gather some back pay. While obviously the street value of the plunder could not have come close to what the Israelites would have actually been owed for their years of service, this was God's way of symbolically settling the accounts. Israel psychologically needed this so as to mitigate the possibility of embittered memories of their Egyptian hosts; the Egyptians needed this, too, as a token way of making right the many years that they had done wrong.

Second, by transferring valuable goods from the Egyptians to the Israelites, Yahweh had now expanded the nation's assets considerably, quite literally *overnight*. As an indentured nation, Israel would have lived on a subsistence level with few discretionary resources to speak of. But now, having been resourced by the Egyptians, each household was able to claim a nest egg of its own. Some of these resources might have been expended after the sea crossing (at least in northern Egypt, archaeologists have uncovered numerous trade posts, the ancient equivalent of all the gas stations, restaurants, and tourist shops we might find off a major interstate exchange in the U.S.). But most of it would have been available for building the tabernacle, a process later initiated by a free-will offering (Exodus 25:1–9). Unfortunately, some of Israel's acquired wealth was also used to form the idolatrous golden calf (Exodus 32:2–4). God was giving to the Israelites means in order that they might in turn give back to God. Although Yahweh obviously foresaw that the Israelites would put their assets to ignoble purposes as well as noble purposes, this did not preempt his graciousness. A good lesson for us all!

Third, I believe that Yahweh was also making a larger theological point—one not necessarily grasped by the Israelites in the heat of the moment—about what theologians sometimes call common grace. Let's just imagine a scenario in which the Israelites had left Egypt completely empty-handed. In that case, they would have come to reflect on their time in Egypt in completely negative terms. Egypt and all things Egyptian would have been viewed with only disgust and hatred. But by prompting the Egyptian hosts to put Egyptian goods in the Israelites' hands—prized pots and vessels with MADE IN EGYPT stamped on the bottom—God was redeeming the memory of Egypt. Notwithstanding the horrors of the cruel bondage, Egypt,

Egyptian people, and Egyptian culture were not *all* bad. Egypt had good elements as well. But that goodness could only be realized as the Israelites took ownership of the raw resources and converted them to good and holy uses.

This is a point worth dwelling on because this is a point that many Christians miss when it comes to interacting with their own host culture. This came home to me one day many years ago when a brand-new Christian in college. I sat down to the piano and just for fun started playing some ragtime music, Scott Joplin's "Maple Leaf Rag" to be exact. No sooner had I hit the final chord, than a Christian brother approached me to dissuade me from playing secular music and to give my talents instead to "Christian music." Of course my friend meant well, but in retrospect I realize that he was utterly misguided. The calling of God's people is not to create our own counter culture that is completely disengaged from surrounding culture (as if that were even possible). Instead, with sober awareness of our own redeemed identity and God's standards of beauty, our calling is to produce culture for the glory of God and to appreciate the "Egyptians" for the good things they produce. Neither uncritical embrace nor wholesale rejection of the broader culture is fitting; a middle way of cautious, reflective appropriation and enjoyment is available. Those outside the church bring some excellent things to the table because they too are created in the image of God, no less than the people of God.

So much for the *why* of the plundering, what about the *how*? Assuming God did not override the will of the Egyptians, somehow forcing them to gift the Israelites against their better judgment, how might we explain their generosity? This too has been a source of some scholarly puzzlement. Some have argued that the Israelite women actually deceived their Egyptian hosts into thinking that they were only loaning out these items on a temporary basis. Although some exegetical proof may exist to back up this position, it does not stand up to historical imagination. Any Egyptian householder, who knew (1) that the Israelites under Moses were petitioning to leave Egypt for good, and (2) that other Egyptians throughout the land were also being asked to pony up, would have known full well that whatever was given to the Israelites would never be seen again.

Another possibility is that Egyptians gave out of a sense of collective guilt for Pharaoh having ruled the Israelites so harshly. This may have an element of truth. (A variation of this is to imagine the Egyptians emptying their pockets out of good will as a way of helping give the soon-to-be former slaves their fresh start.) But perhaps the best option is to suppose that the Egyptians had become favorably disposed to the Jews on account of the plagues. Even if Pharaoh did not honor the God of Israel, most of the Egyptians must have been more than duly impressed by what they had experienced through the outstretched arm of Yahweh. They knew full well that the Israelites' God had vanquished their own gods. So if the Egyptians had been accustomed to making small material sacrifices to their gods over the years, how much more worthy now was the triumphant God of Israel. In giving to the Israelites, the Egyptians would have seen themselves as making a much-needed offering to the priests of Yahweh.

The Quest for a Light-hearted Ending

Israel's God runs interference for Israel in another way, namely, by hardening Pharaoh's heart. A recurring motif in the biblical text and a recurring datum in some longstanding theological debates, the hardening of Pharaoh's heart is expressed by three different Hebrew verbs: *hāzaq* ("to be strong"), *qāshāh* ("to be difficult"), and *kābēd* ("to be heavy"). In some cases, Pharaoh's heart is simply described as hardened (Exodus 7:13, 14, 22; 8:19; 9:7, 35). In other cases, Pharaoh is said to harden his own heart (Exodus 8:15, 32; 9:34; 13:15). Finally, in still other instances, it is Yahweh who hardens the ruler's heart (Exodus 4:21; 7:3; 9:12; 10:1, 20, 27; 11:10; 14:4, 8, 17). Interestingly, although Yahweh announces his intention to harden Pharaoh's heart well before the onset of the plagues (Exodus 4:21; 7:3), he doesn't actually follow through on this promise until the close of the sixth plague (Exodus 9:12). To be clear, before God even becomes involved, Pharaoh's heart was already calcifying. It began hardening even before the plagues (Exodus 7:13–14) and continued to harden prior to and apart from any divine influence (Exodus 7:22; 8:15, 19, 32; 9:7). This process of self-hardening continued in the seventh plague even after Yahweh's very first hardening activity (Exodus 9:12, 34). In the final three plagues, however, Yahweh alone hardens Pharaoh's heart, while the ruler's own autonomous will recedes from view (Exodus 10:1, 20, 27; 11:10).

Two implications follow from this data. First, given the symmetry between God's hardening activity and Pharaoh's self-hardening, we have to rule out two theological extremes. On the one hand, we should not maintain that Pharaoh had no free choice in responding to Moses. On the contrary, Moses himself left open the possibility that Pharaoh would finally accede to his request (Exodus 8:2; 9:2; 10:4), and unless we are prepared to argue that this contingency was nothing more than a theoretical yet unrealizable possibility (whatever that means), a hard-determinism (i.e., God determined everything) reading of the text remains unviable. On the other hand, to suggest that God was an entirely passive agent, merely permitting Pharaoh to make his own poor choices, also will not work. Very clearly, God was personally involved in stiffening Pharaoh's resistance to the divine purpose.

Recently I was reading a popular Christian writer who, reflecting on the notion of God inducing human agents to sin, expressed her opinion that this is "a horrible view of God and a profound *heresy*" (italics original). If this is true, then I suppose it makes the author of Exodus a profound heretic. Although God does not necessarily deal with all human hearts in the same way he dealt with Pharaoh's (though see Romans 9:14–18), the text forces us to hang loose to our philosophical attachments, either to hard determinism or to absolute human autonomy.

The alternating movement between plague and Pharaoh's hardening in the plague cycle not only serves to underscore Yahweh's power, it also makes a point about Pharaoh. This becomes especially clear on appreciating the Egyptian background to the language of hardening. According to Egyptian conceptions of the afterlife, each human soul was destined to stand in judgment before the gods, who would assess the deceased person on the basis of deeds done in the body. If a person did good in life, the result would be a light heart that bore no incriminating testimony against its owner. But if a person did evil, this would result in a hardened or heavy heart. At death, the jackal-headed god Anubis would weigh the heart in the scales against a feather. If the heart weighed no more than the feather, the result would be post-mortem felicity. But if the heart outweighed the feather, the only expectation could be dire judgment, typically involving being fed to man-eating, crocodile-headed Ammut. In the period of the New Kingdom, the dead Pharaoh's survivors would often remove the heart to a canopic jar (a container used in the Egyptian mummification process) and put in its place a fist-sized scarab (a beetle-shaped amulet) designed to serve as a heart that was true. This more or less artificial heart, so it was hoped, would achieve the light-hearted ending every soul—including Pharaoh himself—longed for.

This is a helpful datum, for in stating that Pharaoh's heart was made heavy, the Scriptures are essentially saying—in terms drawn from Egyptian mythological vocabulary—that the ruler of Egypt was storing up judgment against himself. One hardly needs to read between the lines: Pharaoh was not only hardening himself personally against the God of Israel, he was also revealing himself as a moral failure, a state that would be grimly uncovered in the next life. In ancient Egypt, where kings were supposed to embody righteousness and justice, a morally ambiguous Pharaoh was a problem. Through the plagues, Moses demonstrated not only that he was determined to take God's people on the road to the Promised Land, but also that Pharaoh was equally determined to take a highway to hell. In time, thinking Egyptians would draw all the necessary inferences and suddenly the once coherent Egyptian worldview would be on the brink of collapse.

A Unique Plague

I have already noted that the tenth plague was unique in several respects. The biblical writer gives it its own extended space, marking it off as special. It is also quite obviously the only plague that accomplishes what Yahweh had been seeking to accomplish all along: Pharaoh's release of the Israelites. Moreover, the final plague, together with the Passover, marks a transitional stage in the Exodus. As the tenth plague, it obviously belongs with the rest of the plagues; at the same time, it is also the precise moment that the Exodus begins, initiating a protracted process that finally culminates in Israel's conquest of the Promised Land. As such, Passover is a decisive moment straddling tales of both judgment and redemption.

While the plague against the firstborn is similar to the previous nine plagues, it is also significantly different on several levels. First, this is the only plague directly resulting in the loss of human life. In the ancient world, self-perpetuated through primogeniture (the legal right of an eldest son to get his father's property after his father dies), the most devastating family tragedy would be the premature death of the firstborn son. All the other plagues were by comparison mere nuisances. Second, while the first nine plagues were released with intrinsic discrimination against the Egyptians (having no effect on the Israelites by virtue simply of their DNA), this final plague potentially applied to both Egyptians and Israelites. Third, on a related point, this tenth plague required an act of faith on the part of

Israelite householders; that is, if they hoped to be spared, only by sacrificing a lamb or a goat kid (a *seh*) and applying the blood to the doorposts and lintel could the Israelites be saved. For the first nine plagues, the Israelites did not need to lift a finger to be spared; for this plague, they had to smear blood from their own livestock onto their doorposts to ward off the destroying angel of Yahweh. (This is, in fact, how Passover got its name first in the Tyndale and then later in the King James Bible. On seeing the blood, the Lord would *pass over* the Israelite houses. The translation is somewhat erroneous, however, for the Hebrew *pāsah* actually means something closer to "hover" or "stand guard.)

A Covenant Meal

The sacrificing of the *seh* was itself incorporated in a solemn, carefully choreographed meal. This is somewhat different from how most Westerners think of their sacred holidays, where, as important as the meals are to the rhythm of those occasions, they are nonetheless separated from the religious element. On Christmas Eve, for example, people will attend a candlelight service but only eat the holiday meal the next day, typically after all the presents have been unwrapped. On Easter morning, Christians attend church and then go home for Easter dinner, a meal that is detached in time and space from the communal celebration of the liturgical high point of the year. But here, the Passover meal is itself the religious celebration, and vice versa. Eating is transformed into a sacred act.

The fuller significance of the meal does not become clear until Exodus 24, when the Israelites enter into a solemn covenant-making ceremony with the God who saved them. At that time, Moses sprinkles the "blood of the covenant" (Exodus 24:8) on the people, binding them into a formal relationship with Yahweh. Biblical theologians refer to this event as the inauguration of the Mosaic covenant. Here God graciously promises to remain the nation's Lord and Protector, even as he expects the people to respond in obedience. When Moses, Aaron, Nadab, Abihu, and the leading seventy elders of the tribes eat together on the mountain after the covenant-making ceremony, they are recapitulating the act of eating before God that had already taken place on a household-by-household level in Exodus 12. They eat not simply because they are hungry but because, in the ancient Near East, a typical practice for two covenant-making parties would be to share a meal as way of sealing the deal. All this underscores the fact that the inauguration of the Mosaic covenant was not so much to *establish* a relationship between Yahweh and Israel as to formalize an existing one, a covenantal bond that had already been forged through the Abrahamic ceremony (Genesis 15) and now more recently renewed in the Passover (Exodus 12). Even though the finer points of the covenant would be spelled out later at Sinai after the sea crossing, those who partook of the Passover were effectively signaling their own membership within the people of God.

Fast forward to the first century A.D. and we find Jesus drawing on this covenant-making aspect of the Passover when, at his own last Passover meal, he says, "Take. This is my body" (Mark 14:22) and "This is the blood of the covenant which is poured out for many" (Mark 14:24). The very moment he turns to one side to pass the loaf of bread around is the moment at which each disciple must decide for himself, "Am I really all in? Do I dare identify myself as a member of this new covenant that Jesus is inaugurating?" Once each disciple bites into the bread, chews, and swallows, it means nothing less than, "Yes, I am in. I am *all* in." When Christians today take the Lord's Supper, it means the same, nothing less. (Much more is said about all this in my companion book, *Finding Jesus in the Exodus*.)

This covenantal aspect of the Passover meal should strip us of the notion that the blood on the doorpost was a kind of one-off trick to keep the Destroyer at bay and nothing more. Nor should we think of the Passover participants, once on the far side of midnight, as saying, "Phew, close call! Well, got that over with. Now I can get on with my life as I please!" The first Passover ritual signaled a deeper life commitment. By applying the blood and taking the meal together, each household was saying in effect, "Whatever Yahweh requires of us, we as a family are all in." I think that for this very reason, the sons and daughters of Israel are first called a "congregation" here in Exodus 12 and, in fact, are so identified repeatedly (Exodus 12:3, 6, 19, 47). Once a mass of dejected humanity, the Israelites were now a people—the people of God.

A Mixed Multitude

Yet this people was not necessarily ethnically homogenous. From Exodus 12:38 we learn that a "mixed multitude" (KJV) went up with Israel to join in the Exodus. Exactly who this "mixed multitude" was or what motivated them to risk all in order to throw in their lots with Israel is not made explicit. We can safely say, however, that this group was composed of families of non-Israelite descent who, having been impressed by Yahweh's power on display through the plagues, decided to leave Egypt as well. Many of these, we can assume, had a less-than-optimum life in Egypt.

Many of these, we can likewise assume, also participated in the Passover meal. But they had an added cost for such participation: All foreign males would have had to be circumcised, also the standard for later generations (Exodus 12:43–49). This was no easy pre-requisite, at least not for any adult males, for whom circumcision would have been an extremely painful and even dangerous procedure. Sometimes churches talk about being seeker-sensitive. Well, this is a case where joining the worshipping people of God was anything but seeker-sensitive, not when it comes to one of the most sensitive parts of the human male anatomy! Members of the mixed multitude did not decide to join the Exodus lightly. This was serious business requiring real faith.

Venue and Menu

The participation of outsiders should not obscure the fact that the Passover was to be held as a family meal. The basic rule of thumb was one *seh* per family. (It was important that each household match the size of the animal to the size of the family plus the number of invited guests.) The meal was to be eaten indoors within the private space of the family, the basic social unit. Following a prompt from the children, the family leadership was responsible for explaining the significance of the Passover—all in keeping with the Jewish ideal of family-based spiritual formation. From the ancient Jewish perspective, as is evident from the wisdom literature, children were to be nurtured, shaped, and instructed in the ways of God by their parents. (More times than I care to admit, I have witnessed Christian parents abdicating their God-given role when they tell their children's Christian school teacher or youth group leader, "Hey, it's your job to get my children to obey. You're the professionals. Now get to it!")

Once gathered, the meal was actually fairly simple, consisting of bitter herbs, unleavened bread, and the meat. Each of these items had its own significance. The inclusion of bitter herbs was likely calculated to invoke the bitter experience of the Egyptian bondage. This was at any rate how Judaism of the Second Temple period (530 B.C.–A.D. 70) interpreted it. Psychologically speaking, one can see why this symbolic element might be important. Israel would soon face many challenges from this point until the settlement in the land. Whenever difficulties crowd our present experience, we have a way of becoming unduly nostalgic about the alleged "good old days." Indeed, very soon the complainers within Israel would be looking to their past through rose-colored glasses. But the bitter herbs, incorporated into the annual feast as a sober reminder of Israel's darkest days, served to remind the reflecting Passover participants of the depth of Yahweh's mercy. While bitterness has not virtue, sometimes we find spiritual value in keeping a tap-line open to past pain.

The unleavened bread also had its own meaning. In antiquity, wheat or (more typically) barley loaves were staples. Requiring hours of lead-up time, the process of bread baking began at the end of the day, when the bread maker (traditionally the mother) would take a pinch of the previous day's bread dough and work it into a batch of kneaded dough in a small wooden kneading trough. Left to sit undisturbed overnight, the leavened loaf would then slowly rise so that, first thing in the morning, the newly risen bread would then be shunted into the oven. In terms of texture and shape, the closest modern analogy to ancient Jewish bread would be a small flat-crusted pizza with absolutely no tomato paste or toppings. Add a little oil and the spice of your choice, and you would be good to go.

For the purpose of the Passover, Yahweh was asking his people to forego the leavening agent and to bake an unrisen loaf of dough. This would not normally have been the Israelite mother's first choice. (If you have ever eaten hard tack or bread that had failed to rise, you get the idea!) But here the issue isn't taste or texture but meaning. Again, think family road trip where everyone is in a hurry to get on the road. An everyday, situated life has time for extensive kneading and time for letting the yeast do its work. But at this point, the people had no time for such a leisurely approach. Instead, the women were to wrap the loaf in cloth, sling it over their shoulders, and be ready to go. Later, on the road, they would have time to regroup and build campfires where they could cook the unleavened loaves on a griddle or place the dough on heated rocks.

Whatever else we might say about the symbolism of unleavened bread, I would add two points. First, it invoked a collective memory of a situation where everyone had to be ready at a moment's notice. We can only imagine that, as the Israelites were calmly huddled inside houses taking their first Passover meal together, they eventually began to hear noises from outside: the wails and shrieks issuing from the houses of their Egyptian neighbors over finding their children suddenly cold and lifeless. At first, perhaps, just a few isolated shouts would have been heard and from a distance; then, as time went on, a choral cacophony of pain and grief would have risen. Meanwhile, safe inside and protected by the lamb's blood, the family continued to eat and wait for morning when the coast would be clear—to wait for the news of Pharaoh's orders to leave the land. Eventually, when that news came, they performed the ancient equivalent of loading up the family van and joined the throng struggling to organize itself under Moses' leadership. All the while, the mothers had prepared themselves ahead of time by strapping a loaf of unbaked, unleavened bread on their shoulders. The bread symbolized readiness and responsiveness to the Exodus, and by extension to God himself.

Yet the unleavened bread also symbolized that they were a people who were on their way. People who are on a road trip don't have time to linger; they are going places. People who pack bread like this are also people on the go. In this respect, the unleavened bread has a forward-pointing or destination-oriented aspect. Here one might even think of the term "eschatology," the end point to which all of history converges. At Passover, when the Jews would eat unleavened bread, they would be reminded that on the night that they were formed as a people, they were to be a people on the go, a forward-looking people, a people of purpose. To remove this forward-looking, eschatological aspect from Judaism or Christianity is to gut the whole narrative. Passover tells a story that recalls what

God has done in the past and anticipates what God will do in the future.

The central item on the Passover menu was the *seh*, the sacrificed lamb or kid. On the most basic level, the slaughtered animal represents a sacrifice on behalf of God's people. The point was clear enough: The only escape from the destroying angel of Yahweh was through the death of another. This logic would underwrite the entire sacrificial system to be implemented under Moses. Sin was a deadly offense against a holy God and nothing less than blood could secure atonement.

On another level, the *seh* also looks back to the story of the Aqedah (Genesis 22) where Abraham was called to offer his son Isaac as a sacrifice but was instead supplied a ram to offer in his son's place. En route to the mountaintop, Isaac inquired as to the whereabouts of the *seh* that was to be offered (Genesis 22:7). Judaism did not see this as a merely coincidental connection, for the Jews of a later period (for example in texts like *Jubilees* or the Dead Sea Scrolls document *4Q225*) would see a close connection between the Aqedah and the Exodus. For these interpreters, Abraham's horrific trial occurred exactly on the same day as Passover, at exactly the same time—that is, during twilight (thus explaining why in Judaism the Passover lamb must always be sacrificed in the late afternoon or early evening). This Passover date (Nisan 14 = our late March) was also, by the way, the same date as the eve of creation. Accordingly, to identify this date as the fourteenth day in the first month of the newly calibrated calendar year (Exodus 12:2) made sense. This threading of times and dates across redemptive history might seem preposterous to some of us, but the ancient Jews were persuaded that God worked in cycles.

These same readers of Torah had four key nights in the history of Israel, four nights having to do with (re)creation. Three of these nights had already transpired: the night of creation (i.e., the creation of the physical universe), the night of the Aqedah (the creation of the Abrahamic line), and the night of the Passover (the creation of Israel as a nation). The fourth big night, which would also occur on Passover eve, was the night that the Messiah would come (marking the creation of new heavens and the new earth). Thus it is no coincidence that Jesus chose the Passover to announce to his disciples on the eve of his crucifixion: "This is my body broken for you" (Luke 22:19; 1 Corinthians 11:24). For Jesus, this Last Supper, signifying his death and resurrection, was also a moment of new creation.

Although undoubtedly a few scattered households among the twelve tribes stoutly refused to give up their lamb and, in short order, paid the dire consequences, Israel had largely obeyed its God in respect to the Passover. Through this obedience, Israel had proven itself to have followed in the footsteps of Abraham who had been tested by forces of darkness but had obeyed. Now Israel had also been tested and obeyed. Through his obedience, Abraham had shown himself as a true priest, the proven mediator for the salvation of the world. Now through their Passover obedience, the children of Israel had proven that they too could function as "a kingdom of priests" (Exodus 19:6) for Yahweh, even if that functionality would eventually be jeopardized. When I was ordained for the ministry, my friends and family made sure to have lots of food on hand to celebrate; the same applies here in the Passover.

Back in twenty-first-century Chicagoland, in our Chinese restaurant, the last of the sweet and sour pork had been finished off. Having completed our holiday meal, we needed to pay and leave. After all, we had just begun our trip and had a long road ahead. At one time in life I thought that holidays were supposed to be about rest and relaxation, but I've gotten past that myth. Yes, that day was a holiday—but sometimes holidays, particularly those on the road, aren't always restful. The Passover was one such holiday—not particularly restful but a very big day. Marking the birth of a nation and the inception of a new era, Passover pointed back to what God had done through the plagues and pointed ahead to what God would do by planting Israel in the land where, eventually, they would have plenty of time to bake bread in leisure.

In the meantime, they faced a long road ahead. The most daunting bend in the road was, as the Israelites would soon find out, not far ahead.

PASSAGE AND A PEOPLE

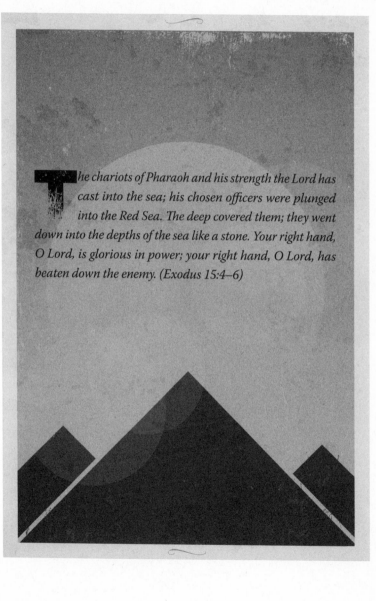

The chariots of Pharaoh and his strength the Lord has cast into the sea; his chosen officers were plunged into the Red Sea. The deep covered them; they went down into the depths of the sea like a stone. Your right hand, O Lord, is glorious in power; your right hand, O Lord, has beaten down the enemy. *(Exodus 15:4–6)*

xiting Yad Vashem Museum and walking along the Avenue of the Righteous, my son and I found a number of trees dedicated to the "righteous among the nations," that is, those Gentiles who distinguished themselves for the Jewish cause during the Holocaust years. Among these is one tree planted in honor of Oskar Schindler and his wife Emilie. Made world famous by the Steven Spielberg film, Oskar Schindler goes down in history as one who managed to save the lives of roughly 1,200 Jews during World War II. He did so by employing them in his enamelware factory and paying off Nazi officials out of his own pocket. A short car ride from the tree, just outside the west wall of the old city near to where we were staying, is Oskar Schindler's much-visited grave. Schindler's final resting place is celebrated because, like Moses, he took great personal risk to save the Jews. Those fortunate enough to have been saved through Schindler's List experienced their own kind of miraculous Exodus. Many are alive today because of sacrificial choices made by one man long ago.

As heroic as Oskar Schindler and others like him might have been, the analogy to Moses is nevertheless imperfect. Schindler had delivered many Jews, just as Moses had. But Moses' work was far greater—greater not only in scope (raw numbers) but also in significance. Today, when people reflect on the meaning of the Exodus, they tend to see it largely if not entirely as a rescue operation, as a saving *from*. But that's only half the story. In reality, it was just as much a narrative about a saving *for* and a saving *to*. From the very beginning of the movement from Egypt, indeed well before it even began, the real story behind the story was Israel's destiny as the people of God. Through the Exodus, Israel was now coming into its own, at least in an anticipatory way.

Purpose

Through the escape from Egypt and the passage through the Red Sea, the nation was on the cusp of fulfilling its calling in three important respects. In the first place, Moses had taken the twelve tribes, constituted by a massive band of dejected slave families, and had given them new *purpose*. In some ways, this sense of purpose was already implicit in the Passover meal, especially in the symbolism of the unleavened bread. By eating this bread, both at the first Passover meal and all subsequent Passovers, the Israelites declared themselves to be a people in a hurry—more exactly, a people on the move focused on a particular goal and destination. But this future orientation was not entirely new even at the first Passover; long before, it was conveyed in the terms of the Abrahamic covenant when Abram was promised that his seed would be a catalyst of blessing for the nations.

Think of it this way. An airline ticket agent who wants to ensure that your bags will be checked through to the appropriate final stop will sometimes ask, "What's your final destination?" The Israelites were not checking their bags into the desert or Sinai; the final stop—the *telos* of their travels—was the Promised Land. All this is bound up in the original call issued to Moses at Sinai, in particular, where Yahweh said: "I have seen the misery of my people who are in Egypt. I have listened to their cry due to their taskmasters, for I know their sufferings. And I have come down to deliver them from the Egyptians and to bring them out of that land *and into a good and broad land, a land flowing with milk and honey*" (Exodus 3:7–8a). The focus on the final destination also emerges in Moses' song of victory, when Yahweh deals with Pharaoh and the Egyptians one last time, once and for all: "You stretched out your right hand; the earth swallowed them. In your unconditional love, you led the people whom you redeemed; *you guided them to your holy dwelling place*" (Exodus 15:12–13). Remarkably, Moses, the very morning after the Red Sea crossing, saw Yahweh as having *already* taken his people to the land of promise: "you guided them"—perfect tense. This can be explained only one way: Because God's purposes for Israel had been so clearly confirmed through the Exodus, the end goal—though still far off into the future—seemed all but a done deal.

Priests

Israel's new purpose ties in with my next point, namely, that Yahweh intended to ordain Israel as a nation of *priests*. In the previous chapter, I argued that when the Israelites requested last-minute handouts from the Egyptians, they were giving the Egyptians the opportunity to pay homage to Yahweh through material goods. There the Israelites were functioning as priests on behalf of Yahweh. This priestly identity was now reinforced in Moses' notation that Israel's final stop would be God's "holy dwelling place" (Exodus 15:13). This appointed cultic space, which included both the land and the temple grounds, served to define not only Israel's purpose but also their cultic identity. Just like a baker who goes to a bakery to express her identity as a maker of bread or like a teacher who goes to a school to fulfill his identity as a pedagogue, so too Israel was called to the one spot on earth where it could finally take on its full priestly identity. Yahweh would put this very crisply in Exodus 19: "So now, if you obey my voice and keep the terms of my covenant, you shall be my treasured possession from out of all the nations. Because the whole earth is mine, you shall be for me a priestly kingdom and a holy nation" (Exodus 19:5–6). Under Pharaoh the Israelites were slaves—nothing more. But under Yahweh, as long as they kept the terms of the covenant, the Israelites would be priests—not just priests but *royal* priests.

Principles

If Yahweh had made Israel a purposeful people and a priestly people, he had also granted the nation a new set of *principles*. By this I mean that he had given them the law. The heart of that law would be explicated in crystallized form in the Ten Words, better known as the Ten Commandments (Exodus 20:1–17). In these ten prescriptive statements, Yahweh summarizes the core of his righteous requirements, entailing both vertical (God-ward) and horizontal (human-ward) orientations. As a priestly nation, Israel needed a proper M.O., a *modus operandi*, an outline of habits and practices appropriate to a holy people. Purpose and priestly identity would be meaningless apart from clear guidelines as to how one goes about doing and being. Israel could not very well function as a priest apart from living a holy life as per the principles of the covenant. Likewise, speaking of God's people fulfilling their God-ordained purpose apart from their priestly identity would be nonsense. Thus, Israel's purpose, priesthood, and principles hang together.

The Call to Passage

Just how all this was worked out on the far side of the Red Sea (that is, once Pharaoh was completely out of Israel's hair) will be treated in greater depth at the end of this chapter. Right now we have to get Moses and his followers to that far side. Through the raising up of Moses and the unleashing of the Ten Plagues, Yahweh had engineered circumstances to ensure Israel's release. But one more piece had to fall into place. Yahweh needed an opportunity to reveal himself so dramatically, so forcefully on Israel's behalf, that no one would have any question as to whether Israel's God was equal to the challenge of making good on his promises. That opportunity came in the passage through the Red Sea.

How Many Made the Passage?

In considering the Red Sea event, we must understand something that I have not yet discussed: numbers. Most people, when talking or thinking about the Exodus, have a vague notion that lots of people were involved. But how many people are we really talking about? Enough to fill a small town high school football stadium? A few of such stadiums? Enough to fill the Rose Bowl? Enough to fill ten Rose Bowls?

Here's good news and bad news. First, the good news is that Scripture actually states a number: "And the sons of Israel journeyed from Rameses to Sukkot, about 600,000 strong men on foot, not counting children" (Exodus 12:37). The bad news is that this number seems outrageously large, making us wonder if the good news (hooray, we know how many) is as good as we first thought.

We need to think this one through. If Israel had 600,000 fighting men, then the total population (i.e., a head count including men, women, children, and infirm men) must have been in the range of two to three million. Again, this is an extremely large number. True, Scripture emphasizes the Israelites' fertility in Egypt (Exodus 1:7–9), but even so, to extrapolate a population growth trajectory from twelve patriarchs (Exodus 1:1–4) to two to three million in the window of only several centuries would be mind-boggling.

Second, a figure of 600k presents all kind of difficulties in imagining the logistics of the Exodus. For example, when the tribes set up camp in the desert, they do so in an orderly arrangement around the tabernacle. But given the dimensions of the tabernacle, this arrangement would hardly be feasible even if the Israelites numbered as few as one million.

Third, in this connection, one might mention the thirteenth-century B.C. Merneptah Stele, discovered in 1896 by one Flinders Petrie (who—small world—happens to be buried in Jerusalem not far from Oskar Schindler). The stele is important in its own right because it is the earliest artifact containing a clear reference to Israel. It is relevant to this question because the verbiage of the stele gives every appearance that Israel was still a small-fry tribe among the much bigger nations. This would hardly be the case if Israel had left Egypt with three million folks, because that would have made them the largest (most populous) nation on earth. Given all these considerations, not to mention many others, we ask, "Could the biblical text be wrong?"

Theoretically, the biblical author could have inflated the number for effect, but I think we have better options for ascertaining Israel's population at the time. The key Hebrew word here is 'eleph, which in the standard translations is interpreted as "thousand." To be exact, there were "600 'eleph fighting men." One possibility is that 'eleph should be translated as "family" or "clan." This is exactly how the same term is used in Judges 6:15, where Gideon says, "My clan ['eleph] is the weakest . . ." (see also Joshua 22:14; 1 Samuel 10:19; Isaiah 60:22; Micah 5:2). In this case, Exodus 12:37 actually reports that six hundred families' worth of fighting men were leaving Egypt. A variation is to suppose that 'eleph means something like "platoon" or "squadron," more or less as we have it in Numbers 1:16, "These are the ones selected from the congregation, the leaders of the ancestral tribes, the heads of the squadrons ['eleph] of Israel." If each squadron ('eleph) represented a corresponding clan, and if each squadron was only constituted by ten or so fighting-age men drawn from each clan, then this is quite a game-changer as far as the numbers are concerned.

Colin Humphreys and Gary Rendsburg, who have written extensively about this subject, take this approach and accordingly theorize that on leaving Egypt, the twelve tribes combined for a population of 22,000–27,500, the size of a small-to-middling-sized American town. In my view, this supposition is as good as any and is surely to be preferred to the mental gymnastics required to make the standard translation of "600,000 fighting men" feasible. Would the total number of Israelites fill twenty-five Rose Bowls? I don't think so. But they could have filled a quarter of that stadium.

Where Did the Passage Occur?

Now that we've settled the numbers question, another issue remains to be resolved: the route by which the Israelites left Egypt. We recall from Exodus 12:37 that the Israelites journeyed from Rameses to Sukkot. Rameses was one of their main work sites; Sukkot, meaning "booths," was probably something akin to a shantytown. Now from here, the itinerary gets complicated and murky. From Sukkot the Israelites reportedly moved on to Etham (Exodus 13:20), but we have no idea where this spot is. The next stopping points are no more illuminating. When Yahweh instructs Moses to set up camp at Pi-hahiroth (from the Egyptian "mouth of the canal"—Exodus 14:2), this likely means a certain point where a canal connects with a larger body of water. The difficulty here is that a portion of Egypt is peppered with lakes with intersecting canals in all directions. (Centuries earlier, the Egyptians had built an elaborate canal system, including a rather long channel running north-south along the eastern border to deter potential invaders.) Ah, but at least we know that this indeterminate Pi-hahiroth is "between Migdol and the sea and in front of Baal-zephon" (Exodus 14:2). Yes, we do know that. But the place name Migdol derives from the Hebrew for "fortress," and more than a few of those stood along the eastern Egyptian border. So far as Baal-zephon goes, we surmise this is a cultic site dedicated to Baal of the North; other than that, we are flat-out clueless. So the route which the Israelites took after Sukkot, at least on this data, is anyone's guess.

The most direct route to Canaan would have been toward the Mediterranean Sea and up along the coastal highway. Of course, here the Israelites would have encountered the Philistines, and precisely for this reason, according to the Scripture, Yahweh redirected them from this route. In God's mind, the sight of the Philistines would send the Israelites fleeing right back into the arms of Pharaoh (Exodus 13:17). Nevertheless, this Bible passage notwithstanding, some scholars have suggested that this is exactly what the Israelites did—they went to the north.

Hans Goedicke is one such scholar. One year before I matriculated as an undergraduate at Johns Hopkins University, Goedicke, its leading Egyptologist, offered a now-famous public lecture on campus. In that lecture, he suggested that the Exodus was the social memory of a catastrophe that started with a cataclysmic volcanic explosion in Santorini Island (off the coast of Greece), dating to circa 1500 B.C. At the time, Moses had led the Israelites on an elevated mount in the eastern Delta, a spot now known as Tell el-Hazzob. On Goedicke's view, they had come there because they had followed the alleged pillar cloud that was actually a plume of volcanic ash hanging over the Mediterranean Sea. Not much later after the Israelites arrived, the dreaded Egyptian army appeared. But just as the Israelites saw the Egyptians coming and sensed that their doom was sure, a tidal wave swept in, seemingly from nowhere, and took out Pharaoh's army, leaving the Israelites—safely ensconced on the hill—untouched. Thus, the enveloping Red Sea wasn't really the Red Sea at all; instead, the deadly waters were the tsunami coming out of the Mediterranean.

I can see why a naturalistic explanation like this is attractive. First of all, it draws on the established fact that around 1500 B.C., the geological record speaks to the biggest volcanic eruption in recorded history—the Minoan eruption of Thera. Second, the theory appears to offer an account of the Exodus that does *some* justice (more on this in a moment) to the text without requiring the supposition of the miraculous. It has, according to one writer who subscribes to Goedicke's hypothesis, shown "that greater credence may be attached to some of the biblical stories than even many biblical scholars have hitherto been prepared to believe."

But hang on a moment. Is this really true? Do we have a compelling reason to prefer this *deus ex machina* explanation (an explanation where the seemingly insolvable is suddenly resolved through some unanticipated and extraordinary intervention) to a more straightforward reading of the biblical account? I'm not so sure. Goedicke's proposal reminds me of a similar resolution to another story recounted in the film, *O Brother, Where Art Thou?* In this movie, the lead character, Ulysses McGill (played by George Clooney), plays an escaped convict on the run from the law. Throughout the movie, McGill is characterized as a staunch rationalist-modernist, consistently putting down the worldview of his admittedly dim-witted accomplices who allow for the possibility of supernatural intervention. In the penultimate scene of the film, a vigilante extension of the law finally catches up with McGill and his cohort in the woods. There the escapees are tied up and about to be summarily executed on the spot, when—spoiler alert, stop reading and skip to the next paragraph if you still haven't seen the movie—lo and behold a tidal wave crashes through the woods, drowning the self-appointed hanging judge and his posse and freeing McGill and his friends as they rise to the surface. Gasping for air and in utter disbelief, McGill's friends are instantly convinced of the miraculous nature of this flood. McGill himself, however, resists this explanation and offers his own patently threadbare scientific explanation for the sudden flood. A quintessentially postmodern film, *O Brother, Where Art Thou?* seems to suggest—against McGill and his rationalist ilk—that some realities simply defy tidy explanation.

My point in mentioning this scene is not to shout, "Hip, hip, hooray!" for the alleged superiority of postmodern epistemology (theory of knowledge) over and against the rationalist tendencies of modernism. My point is rather for us to step back and ask soberly what exactly would be gained by positing a naturalist explanation like Goedicke's, an explanation which, in my view, is not entirely different from that of McGill's in terms of its limited persuasive power. Naturalists who follow Goedicke's line may think they are scoring credibility points by reducing the miraculous element, but here's my question: Does hypothesizing a perfectly timed once-in-a-literal-ten-thousand-years tsunami, occurring *exactly* when and *exactly* where the Israelites needed it (while the Israelites were in turn *exactly* where they needed to be), actually achieve that goal?

Again, I'm not so sure. If in the end Goedicke's theory does not in fact entail a miraculous scenario, then this is surely the most miraculous non-miracle ever.

Now if Goedicke's advocates wish to argue that his proffered scenario, however improbable, is still less improbable than the biblical story, that may be a conversation worth having. But at that point, then, we are merely comparing the relative probability of—as any statistician will tell you without having to think twice—two statistically impossible situations. At any rate, we are no longer talking about a categorical difference between Goedicke's reconstruction and the biblical account but rather about degrees of difference in their respective probabilities—again, technically both variations of nil. In that case, we are better served sticking with the biblical text, which goes out of its way to state that the Israelites did *not* go toward the sea.

One of our few anchor points here is the term *yam suph*, traditionally translated as "Red Sea" in Exodus 13:18. The only problem here is that while we can be certain that the Israelites passed through this body of water called *yam suph*, we can't be entirely certain that the water was the Red Sea. In fact, for a number of decades the reigning hypothesis has been that this was actually a body of water called the Sea of Reeds. Here's why. First, the Hebrew term *suph* is said to derive from the Egyptian word *twf(y)*, meaning "papyrus reeds." This is exactly what *suph* means in Exodus 2:3 and 5, where Moses' chest is nestled among the "reeds" (see also Isaiah 19:6). Second, the Red Sea is a salt water body, but reeds only grow in fresh water. Therefore, *yam suph* cannot refer to the Red Sea. Third, the only reason that *suph* became associated with "red" is on account of a mistranslation of the Greek Septuagint which renders the Hebrew *yam suph* with the Greek *erythra thalassa* ("Red Sea"). This mistranslation was then picked up in Augustine's Latin Vulgate and has been perpetuated ever since. On this view, the translation Red Sea is a big red herring.

But this sea has a leak, maybe a few leaks. First, even if *yam suph* technically means Sea of Reeds or Reed Sea, this does not change the fact that the Scriptures (Numbers 21:4; 33:10–11; 1 Kings 9:26; Jeremiah 49:21; see also Numbers 14:25; Deuteronomy 1:40; 2:1) clearly apply the same phrase to the Red Sea, or its extensions, the Gulf of Suez (jutting up on the west side of the Sinai Peninsula) and the Gulf of Aqabah (jutting up on the east side). That is, in every case the biblical writers intentionally use *yam suph* to refer to a body of water that they know full well does not have reeds.

Second, as Bernard Batto has convincingly argued out, our confidence in translating *suph* at Exodus 13:18 as "reeds" may be misplaced, since a good case can be made for translating *suph* not as "reeds" but as a variant of *soph*, meaning "end" or "extinction." On this reading, the appropriate translation would be neither "Red Sea" nor "Sea of Reeds" but rather "Sea of Extinction." In this instance, too, the epithet *yam suph* would have absolutely nothing to do with any particular water flora but rather with what the water symbolizes: chaos and destruction.

On top of this, Batto further points out that nowhere in antiquity is there a reference—outside of the Bible—to any body of water by the name of *yam suph*. If there were, all would have to agree that

Moses had indeed crossed a Sea of Reeds. So as long as we are missing this piece, perhaps Batto has provided a compelling counter-argument from the biblical text itself. While a number of good solid scholars of various theological stripes hold to the translation "Sea of Reeds" and suggest that the Israelites passed through a lake or perhaps a canal to the north of the Gulf of Suez, I demur. The best read, in my view, is that Moses led his people south to the northern tip of the Gulf of Suez, and then, once cornered by the Egyptians, parted the waters close to that point.

Sea Crossing

The Scriptures inform us that a pillar cloud had led the tribes the whole way. Whatever its physical appearance, the column-like cloud would be all the more awe-inspiring by virtue of what it represented, for the Lord was in the cloud (Exodus 13:21). Moses, Aaron, and the tribal leaders instantly interpreted this as God's leading presence, whether the average Israelite understood it as such—we don't know. I believe so. Ancient Near Eastern mythology is filled with stories of gods who ride on the clouds. Although the Israelites knew so very little about this God to whom they were entrusting their very lives, they would have naturally associated a bright pillar cloud with theophany. The God of Israel was with his people.

"But," the Israelites surely wondered in their hearts, "would that be enough?" We can hardly imagine the swirl of emotions. On the one hand, the cloud, having appeared quite suddenly, must have inspired feelings of gratitude, security, and comfort. On the other hand, we can also imagine the sense of terror the moment stragglers on the rear guard noticed another cloud, a cloud of dust, rising on the distant horizon behind them: Pharaoh's army. In the distance, yes, but also closing in quickly. With the sound of agitated shouts and the sight of arms now intermittently pointing backward, word quickly spread. A collective cry of terror from the back soon made its way like a rolling wave, gathering momentum and volume, all the way to the front—up to Moses and Aaron, who were presumably leading the march at the vanguard as they themselves followed the cloud toward the sea.

On any account, the Israelites were completely cornered. To the rear was the army of a ruthless, vengeful ruler who—in addition to having been bereaved of his son—had been thoroughly humiliated by Moses and his unruly pack of foreigner slaves. No one had any doubt that if Pharaoh could manage to catch up, he would surely take out his pent-up fury on the Israelites and their children. Did they have any hope of out-running Pharaoh? Hardly. With the charioteers leading the charge, Egypt's army was an agile and fast-moving military machine; Israel by contrast could only trudge along no faster than its slowest-moving walkers or pack animals. Could the Israelites turn and fight? This would have seemed equally absurd. The Egyptian force was made up of a fully equipped company of professional soldiers, while the Israelites had no martial training whatsoever (we can be sure that Pharaoh would have officially discouraged such opportunities) and probably very little in the way of weaponry except for clubs and a few swords. Of course, the Egyptian force had numerous other advantages: communication procedures, a well-established chain of command, and most of all, military experience. For any thinking Israelite, the issue wasn't fight versus flight, for neither option was feasible.

Behind the Israelites came a blood-thirsty army; before them stood the sea. Its brooding presence had not only very practical implications (in that it hemmed in the Israelites), it also had symbolic implications.

To understand this, we first have to view the sea through ancient eyes. We may have a cheerful mental image of the seashore where families go for holiday, where bleached-blonde surfers spend their summer days, and where carefree children splash about and make castles in the sand. But for many ancients, the sea was the last place a person would go for personal recreation, much less relaxation. The sea, with its deep associations of chaos, betokened the deep unknown, the demonic, and death. Could the Israelites swim into the sea? The vast majority would not know how. Even for those who could swim, the thought of dog-paddling in the Sea of Extinction would have been psychologically repulsive in a way that we cannot easily understand. To die on the land would be far better than to die at sea, where the body would be lost altogether and deprived of a proper burial.

No wonder the Israelites were plunged into such a frenzy. Some shouted prayers as they pressed forward. Others—the leaders—pulled Moses aside if for no other reason than to express their indignation for having been (at least so they thought) badly misled. The rabbinic tradition relays that at this time the Israelites began gathering rocks with which to stone Moses. The biblical text does not state this, but perhaps it is exactly what happened. After all, if the Israelites could show Pharaoh a dead Moses, the Egyptian ruler might be more inclined to show mercy to his former slaves. Whether through death or life, Moses knew he was on the verge of being deposed.

At this point, Yahweh again instructs Moses to stretch out his arms. As Moses complies, God sends a stiff east wind that blows all night, over time cumulatively driving the water from the basin depth (Exodus 14:21). Apparently, this is not impossible. Russian researchers Naum Volzinger and Alexei Androsov attempted a computer-simulated model of a "wind setdown" (a phenomenon in which a strong and steady wind can move water from one area within a body of water and pile it up downwind) and estimated that 74-mph winds could have possibly exposed an underwater reef in the Suez, thus providing the Israelites a walking path.

More recently, in 2010, Carl Drews (National Center for Atmospheric Research) and Weiqing Han (University of Colorado at Boulder) also presented a workable model for the Exodus, requiring only 63-mph winds. Their investigation presupposed a lake crossing to the north but also presumed, unnecessarily in my view, that the width of the escape route must have been two to three miles in order to accommodate a party that numbered in the hundreds of thousands. But if, as I believe, the Israelites only numbered between 25,000 and 30,000, then this would correspondingly require a path not nearly as wide. (If Drews and Han modified their model to match a narrower path, this would require, in turn, less wind.) The wind-setdown theory strikes me as preferable to the theory of tsunami, not least because it coheres with the biblical account's depiction of a steady wind as opposed to a sudden occurrence. On either version of this reconstruction, other questions remain: How could the Israelites have managed to walk in the face of hurricane-force winds? Would not the basin have had places with extended dips that would require fording or wading through troughs of water? Yes, there are questions, but studies like these are a good start.

As my friend and Wheaton colleague and geologist Steve Moshier will tell you, today's Egyptian coastline is not the same coastline of 3,500 years ago. (Working alongside James Hoffmeier, Steve has done very helpful work in reconstructing the geological landscape of the New Kingdom era.) Sea levels change; sedimentary deposits also change the contours of the ancient map. Indeed, if we contemplate the Suez Gulf in Moses' time, we can see that the salt water extension could actually have come up to the edge of the lakes in the north, which in effect would make the Sea of Reeds versus Red Sea debate almost moot. In short, we have to remember that when we are talking about geography in Moses' day, we are doing a good deal of guesswork.

That said, we might imagine Israel beating across a path that was anywhere between twelve and twenty miles in length—perhaps going as far as two hundred feet below the original water level. On this basis, let's just say that it took the Israelites a good three to four hours (at least) to cross the water basin to the eastern side. As the Israelites made their way to the east side of the shore into the wee hours, they were wondrously grateful for the divinely wrought escape route through the water, but they were nevertheless aware that they were still being followed.

In his determination to bring his slave force back into captivity, Pharaoh had marshaled more than six hundred chariots. This fits the historical record very well. The Egyptians had in fact learned about the usefulness of chariots from their archenemies, the sixteenth-century B.C. Hyksos. By the time of the Battle of Kadesh (1274 B.C.), Rameses II had developed the chariot as a key component of his overall military operation. He would have used—on the assumption of a late Exodus—the chariots as a kind of elite special force. Those in the "chariot division" would be the ones to go in and break down the enemy line, while the foot soldiers behind would follow after and do the mop-up fighting. Chariots made for a good moving platform for longbow shooters, effective in picking off their enemy at great distances. Since longbows were unwieldy on horseback, and a chariot gave the archer room for a virtually endless supply of arrows, even a mere dozen of such chariots approaching the retreating Israelites would have spelled certain slaughter.

The ancient Egyptian chariot had a downside, however. While modern-day tanks do well in various kinds of terrain, the Egyptian chariots—not so much. And this is exactly the point where Pharaoh's chariot unit is undone. As the chariots begin to get jammed with muddy sentiment from the gulf bottom (Exodus 14:25), the wheels begin to come off of Pharaoh's military operation—quite literally. Physically immobilized and psychologically intimidated by the sight of the walls of water around them (the memory of the Ten Plagues was still fresh in many of their minds), the army fell into a panic. At that point, once Israel had safely crossed, Yahweh instructed Moses to stretch out his arms one last time—this time not for salvation but for judgment. The waters came crashing down, and the Egyptians perished. Even if some among the Egyptian chariot riders could swim, many of the drivers and the archers would have been roped to the chariot by the ancient equivalent of seat-belts or body straps. In that case, the water need not have been more than six feet deep.

Ironically, when the contest between Yahweh and Pharaoh first began, Yahweh's snakes had swallowed those of Pharaoh and his magicians (Exodus 7:12); now at the true close of the contest, the sea swallowed Pharaoh's entire army (Exodus 15:12). Much as Pharaoh had given orders to drown the Israelite male infants at the beginning of our story, now at the end of our story came time for Egypt's men to be drowned in the water. Israel's salvation and Egypt's judgment were both accomplished in a single stroke. The Exodus story draws to a close on a note of poetic justice.

In the morning dawn, with the grisly sight of the drowned Egyptians, the Israelites had much to work through, much to ponder. Through God's power they had evaded capture by one of the most powerful military forces in the world. They had successfully crossed the Red Sea by God's intervention alone; they also had looked on as their enemies met a sure destruction—equally by God's intervention. And while they had much to ponder, with some soberness, they also had much to celebrate. The Israelites did so in spontaneous response to God's saving activity (Exodus 15). As the Israelites reflected, they discovered that God had never once expected Israel to do the fighting or to take their destiny into their own hands. Rather, just when the tribes were at the most helpless and vulnerable, God intervened. From that point on, Israel's God would go down in history as the God of the poor and needy.

The Call to Be a People

Now Israel was free, truly free. The wide open desert was before them; the Promised Land awaited. It only remained for the Israelites to follow Moses' lead obediently so that they could realize their God-given destiny as God's chosen people. Yet freedom is not, as so many today seem to think, the ability to do anything we want, depending on our whims or personal cravings. Rather, true freedom is the ability to fulfill the calling that we have been given by God as created and redeemed humanity. Now that God had redeemed Israel through the Exodus, he was also calling them to exercise their freedom according to the purpose, identity, and moral code discussed at the beginning of this chapter. Toward closing, we should consider just how this worked out for Israel.

A Purposeful People

On the morning after the Exodus, Moses led the congregation in a celebratory song of praise. We can think of this as a spontaneous, seaside worship service. The gist of what was celebrated at that service was later reduced into poetic form and now constitutes Exodus 15. In this text, we read Moses chanting the following: "You brought them in and planted them on the mountain of your inheritance, O Lord, which you made to be your abode, the sanctuary, the one, O Lord, which your hands have established. The Lord will reign for ever and ever" (Exodus 15:17–18). As in Exodus 15:13 (discussed above), these verses speak very clearly to the trajectory that Yahweh had mapped out for Israel. Their destiny, their calling, was to establish a place of worship for the one true God, the Creator God. God's temple was also supposed to be the place from which he would reign—the command center, as it were, for the Kingdom of God.

Christians sometimes think that Jesus was the first one to speak about the Kingdom of God. This is simply not true. The Kingdom was already a well-established concept long before Jesus came along. It is a concept that got its start, among other places, right here in Exodus 15. In order for the Kingdom of God to function well on earth, Yahweh had to be worshipped properly by his people. To put it conversely, wherever God's people give God his due, there the Kingdom of God reigns.

Of course, just as we have never had the job of establishing, extending, or building the Kingdom of God, Israel never has either. Notice that the Scripture says it is a sanctuary that *God's* hands have established. God has no interest in watching us go our own way, come up with something we think is brilliant, and then later come back to him with our handcrafted fleshly endeavor and ask him to baptize it. Too often this is how Christians proceed with life. Too often this is how I proceed with life! In either case, it's not right. Only God has the prerogative to establish his work, while our role is to be attentively responsive to his leading. God does not engage us either in our unholy passivity or in our spiritually lazy activism. He engages us through his initiative, his Spirit. From the beginning of redemptive history, the Kingdom has never so much been about what God's people do as about what God has done, is doing, and will do. While much of this is beyond our scope for now (actually I discuss these themes in another book, *Biblical Theology for Life: The Kingdom of God*), the significance of this truth never outlasts our pondering.

A Priestly People

Once in the wilderness, Yahweh called Moses back up to Mount Sinai. Did it seem like another lifetime since his previous visit? For when Moses was last at Mount Sinai, he was but an exile-turned-Midianite shepherd. Now he was something altogether different. Moses was the prophetic leader of Israel, the frontman for the most miraculous rescue operation in history. More than that, he was about to become the mediator of a new installment of the covenant made previously with Abraham.

And this is, in fact, exactly why Yahweh called Moses back up to the mountain (Exodus 19:3)—perhaps Moses suspected as much. In the ancient world, mountains were regarded as having an intrinsic connection with the divine. This is why the Sumerians built their ziggurats—not to show off architecturally, but to establish their own artificial temple-mountain. When God called Moses up the mountain, Moses knew it wasn't for the panoramic view but rather for the purposes of specifying the terms of the covenantal relationship between the Sovereign Lord Yahweh and his vassal people. In short order, Israel was about to be ordained (Exodus 24).

Yahweh began the discussion by reminding Moses how he carried Israel "on eagle's wings" and brought them to himself (Exodus 19:4). Everything that Israel had and everything that Israel had become came from Yahweh. God and God alone was the reason they were free. But freedom without identity or calling is no freedom at all. Yahweh makes Israel's identity and calling more than clear: "So now, if you obey my voice and keep the terms of my covenant, you shall be my treasured possession from out of all the nations. Because the whole earth is mine, you shall be for me a priestly kingdom and a holy nation" (Exodus 19:5–6).

Earlier in this book, I argued that the whole project of the Exodus was to be properly understood within the broader framework of the Abrahamic covenant. In some ways, in redeeming Israel from Pharaoh's bondage, Yahweh was only making good on the promise made to Abram—namely, that Abram's seed would descend to Egypt but then return to the land (Genesis 15:13–16). Now Yahweh had performed as he said he would. He had kept his promise. But the point of Yahweh keeping his side of the covenant was not so much for the sake of Israel but for the sake of the world. Remember, God said that through Abraham's seed all the nations would be blessed, and now this same blessing was to be mediated through the seed of Israel.

Yahweh is not only the God of Israel, he is also the God of the entire world. All of creation is his, and he is its rightful ruler. But in order to establish that rule, in order to bring a creation made unruly through sin and sin's effects back into the creational trajectory, Israel had to play its role. Precisely *because* the whole earth belonged to the Lord, Israel needed to be a kingdom of priests. Their calling was to be a witness and light to the nations. Ideally, once the nations noticed the extraordinary wisdom of this tiny and very ordinary kingdom of priests, they would respond appropriately by repudiating their allegiance to their worthless idols and giving their full worship to the one true God, the Creator God.

One basic way to describe Israel's function as priests, then, is with the term *missiological*. Their mission was to win the nations to God. How would they do it? By representing God to the nations and representing the nations to God. Evangelism, the proclamation of God's glory throughout the earth, is not a New Testament idea—it's an Old Testament idea. By the time the New Testament comes along, God's people get a better idea as to just how to achieve their God-given mandate, but that does not change the fact that the original mandate has roots deep in redemptive history. In truth, it doesn't even start with the Exodus; it starts at creation. To share the glory of God before others is simply to fulfill our priestly role in creation, much as Adam did in the garden.

A Principled People

Once Israel was sorted out as to who they were, they also needed to learn how to live. That leads us to the next step: Yahweh's declaration of the Ten Commandments (Decalogue), or more exactly, the Ten Words. I don't need to list the commandments of the Decalogue here because most readers of this book will know some of them (even if they might not be able to name them all). Spoken, at least by Yahweh's account, not from the mountain but directly from heaven itself (Exodus 20:22), the Ten Commandments are the ultimate summary of God's will for his people. One might say that the remainder of teaching in Exodus, and indeed in the Pentateuch as a whole, is but an unpacking of the principles bound up in the

Decalogue. The well-respected Old Testament scholar Umberto Cassuto once opined that the Decalogue was the climax of the whole book of Exodus. Perhaps he is right.

Notably, the Decalogue was set up within the context of Yahweh's redemptive acts on Israel's behalf (Exodus 20:2). This is an important point because of the way in which the Commandments are often seen by Christians: as points of sheer duty, a kind of punch-list for moral living. While I wouldn't want to deny our responsibility to keep the terms of the Decalogue, I would be remiss not to stress that Yahweh's injunctions were given within a gracious, covenantal context. He did not give us a "to-do" list, walk away, and then say, "Good luck with those. I'll check up on you later." Rather, Israel was to keep the commandments in response to what God had done in saving them. The redemptive order never changes, and our focus should be in keeping with this order: first, on what God has done, and then on what we need to do. When faith simply focuses on our duties apart from our encounter with the living God, it degenerates into legalism and drudgery.

One of the fascinating points about this list of ten command-ments is the fact that while just about everything pertaining to Israel thus far has involved a collective orientation ("you all" or, in the South, "yawl"), here the imperatives are all in the second person singular. Yahweh was addressing not Israel as a corporate entity but each member within the people of God, including Moses him-self. "You *personally* must do this," Yahweh says. God redeemed his people on a corporate level, but then he applies that redemption in such a way so as to require individual responses of obedience. Each of the Ten Commandments is God's unique word for *you*.

Another point of grammar is also relevant—namely, the specific Hebrew rendering of the commandments. Hebrew has essentially two ways to communicate prohibition. One way is to have the negative particle *'al* plus what grammarians call a jussive form of the verb. A second way to give a negative command is through the negative particle *lō* plus the imperfect. The difference between the two constructions is not arbitrary or purely formal, for apparently the two phrasings have a semantic difference. In the case of the *'al* plus the jussive, we are typically dealing with a negative command in a very specific situation. For example, if a Hebrew father is sitting with his teenage son at the dinner table and wishes to express his disapproval of mealtime texting, he would probably use *'al* plus the jussive to say, "Don't text!" In other words, "Don't text right now!" By contrast, the construction of *lō* plus the imperfect denoted a categorical prohibition, a prohibition that was good ever and always. Thus the very same father would use *lō* plus the imperfect in order to say, "Don't text when you drive!" In other words, "Don't text and drive—ever!"

This grammatical tidbit gives us some insight into the Ten Commandments. As it turns out, each one of them is conveyed with the Hebrew *lō* plus the imperfect. This means that God's words in the Decalogue are no one-off. They are binding. For how long? Forever. They are universal, even *eternal* principles. Of course, this raises tricky questions for Christians when they attempt to discern whether Christ had abrogated the Ten Commandments with his own coming. In my view, each of the commandments remains binding to this very day, even if some of them (for example, the command to obey the Sabbath) have been transposed into a different key, as it were. Thus, we should not be surprised when the theologian of grace, the Apostle Paul, recites from the Decalogue (Romans 13:9). He is not saying that the Decalogue is dissolved by the command-ment to love. Rather the love command simply summarizes what God expects his people to do ever and always. If people today say that God's commandments are antiquated, appropriate to an an-cient context but not appropriate for a complex society like ours, I would only answer that ancient Israel was no less complicated (though in different ways). And so far as the applicability of the Decalogue to today's society—well, God thinks they still apply, and therefore so do I.

God remains the same yesterday, today, and tomorrow. The same goes for the Exodus. It was not just an event in the past. The Exodus continues even till this day. God is still in the business of redeeming and renewing his people but more often than not he works through a crisis of passage. Although I am grateful that I for one did not have to experience atrocities of the Holocaust like my grandfather's family did, I have been delivered and still need to be delivered. We are all Israelites.

Yet in another sense, we are all Moses—or at least called to func-tion like Moses. Sacrificing his own interests for the sake of God's mission, Moses had in effect laid down his life for the Exodus. It was a good thing he did so. I have had—albeit on a much smaller scale—my own Oskar Schindlers, my own Moseses in my life. I can only hope I have played something of the same role to others.

Finally, we as Christians should recognize that if our salvation is fundamentally modeled on the salvation of the Exodus (as I hope to show in the next book, I believe it is), then we need to pay attention to just how the Israelites were saved. When we began this book, we found the Israelites in a state of social, political, economic, and spiritual slavery. They were oppressed in all these categories. Likewise, when Moses redeemed Israel, he redeemed them for a fresh start in every way—socially, politically, economically, and spiritually. The Exodus involved the whole package of the human person.

The same is true, I believe, with salvation in Christ. Sometimes Christians will talk about "saving souls" as if human bodies do not really matter. Well, human bodies *do* matter. Just as the Israelites' bodies, battered and bruised under Pharaoh's rod, mattered to Yahweh, so too does the whole person matter to the triune God. This is important. How we think about the nature of salvation will have a direct impact on how we enter into God's mission of saving the world. If we learn nothing else from the Exodus, we learn that God wants to save *whole* people for a *whole* salvation—just as he did for Israel.

As we think about this, we come to realize just why it is so important to have the Exodus revealed before our eyes—again and again. The more we understand the Exodus, the more we will understand what we are to be about. The more we grasp the Exodus, the more we grasp our mission. The Exodus has happened. But a new Exodus is also here. We need to reflect on this with a piece of bread in our hand—and then get moving.

THINKING IT THROUGH

Promise

1. What factors might have led to Pharaoh feeling paranoid about the Israelites and deciding to enslave them?
2. How do we see God's promise to Abraham (Genesis 12:3) being fulfilled in this story?
3. If you were an Israelite slave, how do you think you would feel about God's promise? What might help you hold on to hope?

Prince and Pariah

1. What evidence do you see of God's providential care of Moses?
2. What did Moses learn as a prince about Egypt, himself, and his people?
3. What humbled Moses, causing him to realize that he was a "nobody"? Where do you find your identity?

Prophet

1. What did God use to get Moses' attention? What has God used to get your attention?
2. What did God ask Moses to do?
3. How did Moses try to get out of this assignment? When have you used any of those excuses?

Pharaoh

1. What was Moses and Aaron's strategy for approaching Pharaoh?
2. In what ways were the hand, snake, and staff significant?

3. What was the significance of God's name to Moses, Aaron, and the people of Israel? What does his name mean to you?

Plagues

1. Why do you think Pharaoh had such difficulty in letting the Israelites leave?
2. What did the specific plagues mean to the Egyptians? To the Jews? What was so devastating about the tenth plague?
3. In what ways do people today ignore spiritual reality? What brought you to honor and submit to God?

Passover

1. In what ways is the Passover story "like a bridge connecting the long, drawn-out confrontation with Pharaoh to the Exodus itself"?
2. What does each type of food in the Passover mean?
3. How does the Jewish Passover connect to Christian Communion? In what ways does Communion connect the past and the future in God's story? For you?

Passage and a People

1. What were the three profound aspects of God's calling for his people?
2. How did God deliver the people of Israel when they were trapped between a ferocious army and a threatening sea? When have you felt as though you were in a similar trap? How did God deliver you?
3. Why were the Ten Commandments so important for the Israelites as they lived out their identity as God's people? Why are they important for you?

ADDITIONAL READING

Batto, Bernard F. "The Reed Sea: *Requiescat in Pace*." *Journal of Biblical Literature* 102 (1983): 27-35.

Cassuto, Umberto. *A Commentary on the Book of Exodus*. Jerusalem: Magnes, 1967.

Currid, John D. *Ancient Egypt and the Old Testament*. Grand Rapids: Baker Books, 1997.

Davis, John James. *Moses and the Gods of Egypt: Studies in the Book of Exodus*. Grand Rapids: Baker, 1971.

Erman, Adolf, *Life in Ancient Egypt*. New York: Dover, 1971.

Hoerth, Alfred J. *Archaeology and the Old Testament*. Grand Rapids: Baker, 1998.

Hoffmeier, James Karl. *Israel in Egypt: The Evidence for the Authenticity of the Exodus Tradition*. New York: Oxford University Press, 1997.

Hort, Greta, "The Plagues of Egypt," *Zeitschrift für die Alttestamentliche Wissenschaft* 69 (1957): 84-103.

Humphreys, Colin J. "The Number of People in the Exodus from Egypt: Decoding Mathematically the Very Large Numbers in Numbers I and XXVI." *Vetus Testamentum* 48 (1998): 196-213.

Rendsburg, Gary A. "An Additional Note to Two Recent Articles on the Number of People in the Exodus from Egypt and the Large Numbers in Numbers i and xxvi." *Vetus Testamentum* 51 (2001): 392-396.

Shanks, Hershel. "The Exodus and the Crossing of the Red Sea, According to Hans Goedicke: Leading Scholar Unveils Evidence and Conclusions." *Biblical Archaeology Review* 7 (1981): 42-50.

Shaw, Ian, *The Oxford History of Ancient Egypt*. Oxford; New York: Oxford University Press, 2000.

Sivertsen, Barbara J.,,. *The Parting of the Sea : How Volcanoes, Earthquakes, and Plagues Shaped the Story of Exodus*. Princeton: Princeton University Press, 2009.